Grass Roots
Humanism

dh
Devonshire House

Published in 2001 for Devon Humanists by
Devonshire House Christow Exeter Devon EX6 7LU
(e.mail: dev.house@eclipse.co.uk)
Profit from direct sales of this book will go
to Devon Humanists' Education Fund.
Devon Humanists is affiliated to
the British Humanist Association
charity number 285987.

British Library Cataloguing in Publication Data.
A catalogue record for this book
is available from the British Library.

ISBN 0 9524513 44

Printed and bound in Great Britain by
Sprint Print Exeter Devon EX4 1AY

Inside

(Letters a-i follow a brief chronology of the development of Humanism.)

(Letters a-i follow a brief chronology of the development of Humanism.)

Preliminary

Each of the pieces in *Grass Roots Humanism* can generate ideas. And ideas are what Humanism is about. They come through exploration of the mind, stretching thoughts in many directions.

Greek philosophers did that when they went against current thinking and argued, discussed and questioned. Their ideas can be seen as early roots of Humanism and are briefly shown in *Early philosophy:humanist thought* (see page 41). But Humanist roots go further back than that if we look at the origins of morality.

A moral code developed long before Moses and the ten commandments, and long before the earlier laws of Hammurabi, depicted on two stone tablets which date from before 1750 BCE. The basic necessity of primitive people to live in harmony, in order to survive, would have produced some form of moral conduct (see page 10).

Although both religionists and Humanists share this need for a moral code, they differ over its source. And both believers and non-believers in a god feel a need to express appreciation for the world in which we find ourselves living, but we address our appreciation and thanks in different ways.

Humanists are thankful that we are the product of the billionth/trillionth chance of germination and survival, so we appreciate the life we've acquired and want to help others to do the same. Religionists recognise this too, but they thank a god or gods that embody all the unknown answers.

Time has given us some of those answers, but the ultimate answer to 'Why are we here?' remains elusive. Humanists say we don't know, because it is a question that goes back to the unknown and, with present knowledge, the unknowable.

Religion embraces a perception of life beyond reality, which Humanists are unable to accept. At the same time, Humanists appreciate the need for a framework and that many people find that framework in a religious belief.

That is the dichotomy, because many believers, who do not examine their beliefs too closely, are anxious to propound them without wanting to consider an alternative view. And whereas some religions believe in evangelising, a Humanist attitude develops through experience of life and a process of rational thought. If questioned, Humanists are happy to explain their views, which may initiate discussion. But the dilemma for Humanists is in understanding that many people with religious convictions *need* that belief. It becomes a part of them and I, certainly, would not want to undermine that perception if it is needed in this way.

My own journey to Humanism may have been influenced by my father's strong religious belief contrasting with my mother's ex-Methodist and increasingly rationalist views. But the major turning point came in my early teens when I was taught History and Religious Knowledge by the same teacher. The whole class engineered and sidetracked both lessons into 'discussions' on religion. They usually became quite heated because we were at an age when we questioned everything.

I even studied the bible at home, finding many discrepancies to use as 'ammunition' with which to bombard the unsuspecting teacher. Many points which had brief or no reference in the bible, but had later become doctrine, were argued to our satisfaction. Many implications of conflicting accounts were fiercely discussed. Many irrational happenings were contested. In the process, I came to view the bible with greater interest because it showed me that accepted religious views could be questioned. I also learnt that the roots of religious belief go way back before biblical times, and that our knowledge is continually changing as more fascinating archaeological finds are made. By putting 'modern' religion in context with primitive beliefs, I began to trace a progression of thought from those early civilisations.

That was the start of a lifelong interest in religion, not as a believer, but as a 'researcher' asking myself questions, delving into books and later studying theology at Exeter. But long before my studies, I came across a book which I continue to treasure, *The Humanist Frame*. Suddenly, here were all my partially formed non-religious beliefs set out in essay form by eminent writers and philosophers — I was no longer alone in my thinking! In the copy my husband gave me he wrote, '*Now other library users can borrow the library copy!*' Fascinated to find a book that expressed 'my' ideas so succinctly, I soon found out more about Humanism before joining the British Humanist Association (BHA) in 1966.

It seems fitting that I should start this miscellany of Humanist thoughts and attitudes with a quotation from *The Humanist Frame*. Sir Julian Huxley, who edited the collection of essays and who was the first president of BHA, UNESCO and the United Nations, gave his own reasons for developing humanistic ideas. In his preface, Julian Huxley wrote that it was no sudden venture, but the natural outcome of a long process of over half a century of thought reconciling and integrating various aspects of his life:

> ... my biological training, my twin loves of nature and poetry, my wrestlings with the problems of morality and belief, ... continued in the effort to extend the concept of evolution over the widest possible range of phenomena.
>
> *Sir Julian Huxley, The Humanist Frame 1965 Allen & Unwin.*

Many of the pieces in this present collection are from *Humanist Forum* which is issued four times a year to members of Devon Humanists. Some I have altered, adapted or enlarged for the different format. Others were first printed in Humanist newsletters, books and literature and some pieces have been specially written. But all express Humanist attitudes and give a flavour of grass-roots Humanism.

Humanism is worldwide, but lack of space allows only a few representative countries to be included. Similarly, only a few books and 'valued lives' of interest to Humanists are briefly described. With so wide a range of subjects, chronological order would give an imbalance to the collection. Hopefully the 'jumps in time' and changes of theme will add to its diversity. (For a brief chronology of the history of Humanism follow pages: 9 10 12 41 47 59 73 16 19).

My sincere thanks to all who have helped to make this collection possible, particularly to the contributors listed below. Corresponding initials are shown at the end of each item and contributors' details are given on page 90. Those uninitialled are MS.

PA Peter Astwood; **MB** Maureen Berry; **RB** Roy Brown, **BB** Brenden Butler; **KC** Kate Contos; **JE** John Eadle; **MG** Martin Gilbert; **NG** Nigel Green; **JL** John Langford; **RL** Richard Lovis; **RM** Roger McCallister; **CM** Carole Mountain; **MN** Margaret Nelson; **SP** Stephen Park; **RP** Richard Paterson; **HQ** Henrietta Quinnell; **CR** Claire Rayner; **BS** Barbara Smoker; **BSt** Bryan Steane; **BT** Bob Tutton; **JWW** Jane Wynne Willson.

Margaret Siddall
Christow Devon 2001

What is Humanism?

"How did life begin?"
"Why do we exist?"
"What happens when we die?"
Questions, questions, but what are the answers?

Humanism is a means of finding some of the answers —
not based on the existence of a god or gods, but on rational
evidence from human experience and from scientific
knowledge.

Humanism is concerned with the care of humanity and the
natural world. It is not just 'non-religious', it is a positive,
rational outlook based on natural order not *super*natural or
divine intervention. It means judging situations and people
on their merits by standards of reason and humanity.

Humanists believe that co-operation and individuality are
equally important. They try to live full and happy lives and
by their actions help others to do the same during their
lifetime. When they die, that is the end of that life. But
family traits continue and memories and example live on.

With present scientific knowledge, Humanists believe it is
not possible to know how life began, nor can we foresee
what may happen in the future. People, as a species of the
animal kingdom, have evolved over billions of years. We
now find ourselves to have intelligence and skills that place
us in a unique position over the planet.

We have no intrinsic right to our powers, it has just turned
out that way. But because we can analyse and realise the
consequences of our actions, everyone has an enormous
responsibility, not only in helping to create fulfilled lives, but
in safeguarding the future of life and the environment.

Origins of humankind

It's hard to imagine the time span of two million years, when human-like beings were emerging from their ape-like ancestors.

Before this time, fossil records show that different branches of developing ape-like creatures existed along side each other. But the greatest change came around five to ten million years ago with bipedalism. Why our early forebears, and others that ultimately became extinct, stood on their hind legs no one knows, but many reasons have been put forward.

One reason is that with climatic changes food became scarce, and it was less cumbersome to move around on two legs in search of food. Another is that by standing up, creatures were better able to see impending danger — in the same way that meerkats do today. Whatever the reason, a branch of ancestors stood, and in standing and walking their abilities increased.

The shape of these early fossil skulls shows the altered position for the spinal cord would have enabled an upright posture, yet the skull itself shows apelike features. Some time before 2.5 million years ago the first large brained human species evolved. The shape of the skull had changed and the teeth showed an adaptation to a mixed diet. But these changes took place over millions of years, and continued as prehistoric human, *homo sapiens*, emerged as a separate species.

Arguably, three major revolutions mark the history of life on earth. The first was some time before 3.5 billion years ago, when micro-organisms became a powerful force in the world. Secondly, about half a billion years ago, came the evolution of multicellular organisms. And thirdly, within the last 2.5 million years the emergence of human consciousness. 'Life became aware of itself and began to transform the world of nature to its own ends.'

This remarkable story, detailed by Richard Leakey in his book *The Origin of Humankind*, shows fossil discoveries that have helped to unravel the amazing stages of evolution alongside biological changes that have appeared. The development of mind, language and art all take their place in this continuing story of our knowledge. No book can give all the answers, but this one goes a long way in mapping out our progress so far.

(The Origin of Humankind by Richard Leakey see Bibliography on page 92)

Morality began with the herd

"What is the basis for Humanist morality?" many people ask.

The basis for *all* morality is the need to live in harmony within a community. This basic concept goes back to the time when the first primitive beings started to live in groups, at first in families, then in larger communities. Although the idea of immorality, as opposed to morality, may not have been apparent, it would have been necessary for an underlying basis of a moral code to have developed.

Human instinct, as animal instinct, is concerned with self-survival, but through necessity self-survival also means co-operation with others. This in turn leads to individual and group survival, which can be seen in many instances in animal behaviour. From the simplest form of interaction a 'moral code' would have emerged within the earliest communities and been handed down through the ages, developing recognised good and bad behaviour patterns.

The Golden Rule of 'do as you would be done by' is variously described by all the ancient civilisations. At first it passed down verbally before being written into ancient laws such as those of Hammurabi. Later, it came to be included in the Torah as part of Jewish doctrine, and later still it was quoted by Jesus. But its origins are embedded in the need to live in harmony together.

Morality began with the herd, because individual innate selfishness (the instinct to survive) had to adapt to the needs of nomadic groups or 'herds', otherwise the individual within it would not survive. Each member would have needed to offer some benefit to the group in the division of work or skills.

This simple concept was borne out when details of the wild boy of Avayron* came to light in 1800. When the boy was found, his focus was totally on food, sleep and shelter for survival, because he had been living on his own. As he was encouraged back into society, he gradually learned that being aware of others, co-operating and finally helping them, his needs were also met.

Morality, although intrinsically tied in with 'self', prevents people from remaining at the level of the Wild Boy through indulging only selfish desires without considering other people.

*(The Forbidden Experiment by Roger Shattuck see Bibliography page 92.)

Not just terminology

Is there a difference between Humanist and humanist? Surely all humans are humanists?

> Essentially, we are all fundamentally involved with the hopes, aspirations, sadness, complexities and vicissitudes of what it is to be human. We are humanists when we care for others, when we cry in joy or in grief, when we share the experiences of others, when we want to help people, when we feel sorry for people, or even when we identify with heroes or heroines ... To be truly human we have to be humanist. *Jeaneane Fowler*

In the same way that someone can have liberal views and not be a Liberal, or catholic tastes and not be a Catholic, someone can have humanist attitudes and not be a Humanist. But although those with religious views can have humanist (humanitarian) attitudes, they ascribe the basis of their humanity to reasons other than natural or human-centred ones.

Simply put, the capital H in Humanism denotes the body of thought which rejects divine intervention as the basis of our origin and purpose, and replaces it with a belief in the interdependence of humankind and the natural world. Humanism is therefore not a religion, but a life-stance.

To complicate issues still further, religions are life-stances, too, which give meaning to their adherents' lives in the same way that Humanism does for Humanists. But whereas religions are generally mono- or polytheistic, with supernatural elements, Humanism is non-theistic. Humanists do not worship a 'higher being' or profess belief in the supernatural.

Taking this train of thought further, agnostics and atheists are non-religious. But not all agnostics and atheists are Humanists because not all believe in the basic tenets of Humanism, whereas all Humanists are either agnostic (it cannot be proved that a god exists) or atheist (there is no god). It is not just a question of terminology. There are deeper, fundamental differences between 'natural' and 'supernatural', and how we view humanity, because Humanism is concerned with this life, not a projected and hoped for life in the future.

(Humanism by Jeaneane Fowler see Bibliography on page 92.)

Total eclipse

Anyone who has witnessed a total eclipse of the sun cannot help being overwhelmed by its effect — the gradual darkness, the silence as all the birds stop singing, then the slow return of the light. Even with a cloudy sky, the effect is awesome.

Imagine how such an event would have frightened early man. Subsisting close to nature they knew about seasons and used simple astronomical references to measure them. The quality of their crops depended on the weather, and the sun became an early focus of veneration. Then, one day, the sun disappeared. Something had swallowed it! But after much crying and wailing it returned. 'Blessed be the sun.'

Folk tales developed to explain eclipses. In China a dragon was supposed to have swallowed the sun and the subsequent ritual dances made the dragon spit it out again. In North Africa, groups shot burning arrows into the sky to rekindle the sun's light.

Many societies had sun-gods. The Incas had Inti, the Aztecs had Tonatiuh, while the Hittites had a sun-goddess. The Japanese thought the Mikado was descended from the sun, which they still depict on their national flag. The Egyptians believed the Pharaohs were descended from the sun-god Horus, who was the strength of Ra, the sun-god and creator. The body of Ra was Aten, represented by a flat shining disc. The Sumerian's sun-god was called Shamash, who was 'the one from whom no secrets are hid'. In Babylon the symbol of Shamash was a disc with a four-pointed star and rays of light coming from it. The Romans depicted Jupiter and Apollo with haloes, and kings wore golden crowns to invest them with divine authority. Golden haloes around the heads of pagan gods are seen on early mosaics and sculpture.

The story goes that it was not until the seventh century that Christian effigies wore haloes, when outdoor statues of saints were given circular horizontal haloes to stop the birds defacing them. But early sun-discs, showing divine status, have been perpetuated through the years as haloes in many religious paintings.

This star that our tiny planet orbits enables life to flourish. All our energy comes from it. No wonder it has always been worshipped. To the present time, Sunday, a day of the sun, is a special day for Christian worship. *PA*

You are in my world

There are millions and millions of worlds. Each individual is surrounded by an unseen bubble of his or her particular world, with its own unique structure of connections. Two worlds may be closely entwined, but they cannot be the same or be known completely from another person's perspective. Nor can they be totally subsumed within each other, because 'I' and 'me' and 'mine' will always predominate.

Babies look out on their new world and see objects which, to the baby, no longer exist when they are out of sight. Then comes school, a major part of the growing child's life. But at first children are so absorbed with their own world that 'school' and 'teacher' have the same image. Only gradually do teachers emerge from this perception as other worlds begin to be realised. School now becomes one of innumerable interconnecting worlds to which individuals, including teachers, belong.

Overlaid are the teeming worlds of family connections, places of work, countries, religions, philosophies, sports and other social groupings. Later still come the worlds of commerce, finance, 'consumerism' and politics. Each world brings with it its own particular set of behaviours and expectations. And all the while we enrich our own world by absorbing aspects from other people's, in the same way that our characteristics impinge upon them.

If a video camera could catch the intricacies of involvement that influence our lives, it would be mind expanding. Even snatches of overheard conversations may influence our thoughts or actions. But we are seldom aware of the many minor details from 'other worlds' that we subconsciously retain.

Look at people walking along a road. Where have they come from? Where are they going? What are they *thinking?* Each one is concerned with his or her world, yet without realising it being a part of so many more. We move temporarily in and out of many people's perception, as we influence or are being influenced, sometimes by the briefest inclusion, before moving on.

The problem with humanity is realising the complexities of these other worlds and, by so doing, understanding a little of the worlds to which each person belongs.

Why I'm a Humanist — 1

I am lucky in having been brought up a Humanist. In fact I'm a second generation Humanist. My father was a traditional atheist — what's all the fuss about religion? But my mother, Margaret Law Smith, was more of an agnostic, extremely thoughtful and interested in the potential in the reasons for human spiritual needs. Both parents believed in children having religious education, both to make sure we were not treated differently at school, and more so to make us understand the place of Christianity in the development of modern culture and ethics.

Two points stand out from my childhood and Christianity. Firstly, the comfort of my mother explaining that it was all just outgrown legend after the vicar's dose of hellfire on Thursday mornings. And conversely my mother's approach to Christmas — a time to celebrate the good in life, introduced on Christmas Eve by the stable story read from *The Bible Designed to be Read as Literature*.

I have always been interested in the past and archaeology, and have been closely involved in the latter since the age of fifteen. In reading and thinking about the variety of ways in which human beings develop and express their non-material needs — for ceremony, mental security, understanding the cosmos, even for excitement — I have been increasingly struck by the way in which people the world over make 'religion' in their own image, to suit their environment and way of life, and not the other way round.

In adult life, I have never had problems of seeing all things which get described as religious arising out of basic human needs. In middle life, the death of my mother in the early eighties, forced me to confront head-on the pseudo-religious establishment of modern English life. The difficulties in arranging a Humanist ceremony for her focussed my mind on the need for these, and led me to a period in which I acted as an officiant.

Amongst other satisfactions, it provided a quiet yet positive way of affirming and making known Humanism. The major challenge Humanism now faces is demonstrating that it is a positive, ethical way of living, and not just materialistic escape. The important thing for everyone who is a considered Humanist is to let people know. Humanists come out! They must be everywhere. *HQ*

Valued lives
Charles Darwin —*1809-1882*

Charles Darwin was born in Shrewsbury, educated at Shrewsbury Grammar School and studied medicine at Edinburgh where he also furthered his childhood interest in natural history. He went on to Christ's College Cambridge and continued his biological studies more seriously, concentrating on zoology and geology.

Darwin eagerly accepted the unpaid post of naturalist to the Admiralty's scientific survey of the eastern coast of South America. Captained by Robert Fitzroy, HMS *Beagle* set sail in 1831 with the main tasks of making maps and measuring longitude. The five-year voyage, to areas little known to European naturalists, turned Darwin into an acknowledged expert on natural history and geology, enabling him to make scientific observations and collect specimens of exotic plants, animals and insects.

Each day, Darwin wrote up a record of his discoveries, and his intense feelings on arrival at each new place. He regularly sent these pages home to his family, and soon after returning to England completed his first book from this detailed diary. *The Journal of Researches* was published in 1839, the same year in which he married his cousin, Emma Wedgwood. They moved to Kent where Darwin furthered his practical knowledge on plant and animal variations and interbreeding. While he worked on theories of the origin of species, he 'allowed himself to speculate' before making conclusions, embodying the theory of natural selection. His caution in delivering his findings was because they completely overturned accepted religious views of creation.

After receiving a paper with similar ideas from Alfred Russel Wallace, Darwin was persuaded to condense his mass of notes and publish his findings. *The Origin of Species* was published in 1859, when his epoch-making work was both violently attacked and vigorously defended, finally being accepted by most biologists. Darwin continued to work on a series of treaties, but his theory that the human race was descended from lower forms of animal caused the greatest controversy. Although Darwin was not the sole originator of the principles of evolution — Erasmus Darwin and Jean Lamarck had each worked on the evolution of plants — Darwin's travels, discoveries and ability to extend his ideas, enabled his findings to become theory and not hypothesis.

Ethical Union

In the last decades of the 19th century many ethical societies were founded. Felix Adler started the ethical movement in America in 1876, and ten years later it was brought to Britain by Stanton Coit when the London Ethical Society was formed. The main purpose of Ethical Societies was to 'disentangle moral ideals from religious doctrines, metaphysical systems and ethical theories' (*Blackham*). They also provided an independent force in personal life and social relations. It was not intended that the movement should attack the churches nor be in competition with them, but to establish an ethical outlook and foundation for social reform.

The societies were involved with moral education, penal reform, and neighbourhood community work. They also assisted the woman's movement and called attention to racial, colonial and international problems by initiating and supporting effective action. In 1896 the Ethical Societies in England formed a union, and this was incorporated in 1928 as the Ethical Union.

(Humanism by Harold Blackham see Bibliography on page 92.)

* * * * *

Potted profile — 1

While still at school the idea of evolution kindled the imagination of Julian Huxley, who continued the interest of his grandfather, Thomas Huxley, and the outstanding part he had played in publicising Charles Darwin's theory. As an undergraduate, Julian Huxley became a firm 'Darwinian' and as a young teacher the first public lectures he gave were on evolution. In the 1930s he worked in political and economic planning on varied projects including the place of arts in national life and the world population problem. After the second world war, his work with UNESCO showed him 'what a vast quantity of knowledge was lying around unused'. These were some of the factors which resulted in his belief in Humanism for, as he wrote, 'Human knowledge worked over by human imagination is seen as the basis of human understanding and belief, and ultimate guide to human progress.'

(The Humanist Frame Editor Julian Huxley see Bibliography on page 92.)

What is the soul?

The futuristic prospect of cloning a human being has forced buried questions about body, mind and soul out of the realms of fantasy. But how can a soul be cloned? What does the word 'soul' really mean? Is it another way of saying self or the psyche? It has been suggested that, although the soul cannot be found in DNA as our DNA contains 'the story of life' it has to contain the soul. Therefore it must be 'in the invisible gap that separates the codons of DNA' *(Deepka Chopra Sunday Times)*.

As a child, there were many questions I wanted to ask about the soul, but I didn't ask them because they would have appeared frivolous. I wondered about evolution and humans developing from animals, and whether animals had souls. If they did, I wanted to ask, how did we know? And if they didn't, at what stage of evolution did souls suddenly appear?

The questions are still relevant today because we are left with the question, what *is* the soul? And now, how can it be identified 'in the gaps of DNA'? A quick look in a variety of recent dictionaries shows that along with definitions such as 'the vital principle that moves and animates all life' and 'a human being', each dictionary has one entry that shows *soul* as an entity in itself, 'the immortal part of man'; 'disembodied spirit of a man'. But I was delighted to see that my 1900 *Chambers Etymological Dictionary* gave no such supernatural definition:

> ... that part of man that thinks, feels desires etc.; the seat of life and intellect; life essence; internal power; energy or grandeur of mind; a human being; a person.

It seems that the word 'soul' has changed its emphasis in the last 100 years, possibly because even before the secrets of DNA started to be unravelled it was easier to say the soul lives on, rather than the whole person. But DNA has changed that, particularly when buried questions have come to the fore. What happens to clones and identical twins? Do such pairs share a soul that is already encoded? A rational view may be that the word 'soul' is a way of expressing the essence of an individual life. It is created by the synergy of mind and body, tempered by environment. So without mind, body and environment 'the soul' cannot exist.

17

The thinking machine

Wherever we look we find examples of the many awesome physical feats performed by the different animal species. We marvel at their highly developed range of senses, their intricate skills, the incredible way they have adapted to their unique environments and their ability to survive. Humankind can only wonder at such untaught accomplishment, such incredible cleverness. And yet humans are set apart from these remarkable creatures and are placed at the top of the animal tree. But although we share many of their physical characteristics and behaviours, we have gained our position of dominance through the evolution of our *language* and *thinking*.

To account for the chance development of superior mental powers in *homo sapiens*, a recent theory suggests that the need to communicate developed through grooming routines of primates, who lived in particularly large social groups. It is obvious that communication takes place within and between species, and claims have been made that gorillas and chimpanzees are able to use language to communicate with humans. People also say their caged birds can be taught to talk and that other pets can 'understand' and respond to them orally. But human *thinking* frees us from using our oral abilities in this purely instinctive and stimulus-bound way or from simply imitating others.

Between the ages of four and seven, children develop a reliable logicality as their mental life is no longer dominated by perception alone. By their teens an entirely new, mature, adult way of thinking is beginning to develop which has its roots in earlier phases of childhood. At this time most young humans start to acquire the ability to hypothesise and reflect in the abstract (often called *propositional* thinking). Whereas all children develop a logicality at a concrete level, the degree to which they go on to think effectively in a *propositional* way depends on the practice they have in their own particular social and cultural environment.

The attainment of this prized human goal, an achievement which sets us apart most starkly from the animal world, is greatly enhanced by language that inevitably develops when relating with others about knowledge, ideas and values: thought stimulating language and language stimulating thought. *NG*

Background to the —

British Humanist Association

If it wasn't for the many strands of humanist/rationalist/secularist thought that were coming together, it could be said that an irony of name enabled the British Humanist Association (BHA) to be formed. Back in 1962, the British representatives at the annual conference of the International Humanist and Ethical Union (IHEU see pages 33-4) did not represent an organisation entitled 'Humanist'. Even though there were many local and university Humanist groups in Britain, the overall national body that had contact with them was the Ethical Union (EU).

A Humanist Council had been set up in 1950 which loosely linked the major freethought/secularist movements. But the Rationalist Press Association (RPA see pages 59-60) and EU were more closely allied and formed the Humanist Association in 1957. This was an interim organisation before BHA was put on a firm footing in 1963. The two organisations retained their own identities: EU in West London was concerned with public relations, and RPA, in Drury Lane, with publishing, but each used their respective facilities and resources to promote BHA:

> An inaugural dinner was held in the House of Commons in May 1963 with Sir Julian Huxley, the first president, in the chair. There was an immediate response, and a steady accession of members strengthened local groups affiliated in the EU and formed new local Humanist groups. About the same time, Humanist groups which had been formed in the universities were brought together and instituted the Humanist University Federation. *from Humanism by H.J. Blackham*

As vice-president, A.J. Ayer took over the presidency from Julian Huxley, with Baroness Wootton becoming the new vice-president. Harold Blackham remained the Director for many years and was a leading force in the organisation. The advisory council to BHA had fifty-four members including: Prof Herman Bondi, Dr J. Bronowski, Prof H.J. Eysenck, Sir Gilbert Flemming, E.M. Forster, Dr James Hemming, Sir Julian Huxley, Margaret Knight, Yehudi Menuhin, Bertrand Russell, Lord Willis. . .

With this backing BHA was established. At first, membership included automatic membership of the two parent bodies, with regular copies of *Humanist*, the monthly journal of RPA,

Humanist News, issued ten times a year, and *Rationalist Annual*. The machinery of EU was also used to help form new local groups. But in 1965 organisation of BHA by EU and RPA was to end. Because of the charity laws EU was removed from the register on a technical point. Long battles were to ensue. In the meantime it necessitated RPA, because of its own charitable status, pulling out of the joint running of BHA.

EU continued until 1967 when it was subsumed within BHA, who remained in EU's prestigious building. The battle for charitable status continued and was eventually won in 1983.

From the start BHA was involved with many issues including:

* the publication of pamphlets, books and periodicals, arranging conferences and courses, promoting campaigns and forming local Humanist groups;
* calling for and promoting new thinking, research and experiment in moral and religious education;
* helping Humanist parents and teachers with the problems in which their position involved them at home and at school;
* seeking a fuller and fairer representation of Humanist views in broadcasting and the press.

Being internationally minded, BHA is linked with Humanists throughout the world through IHEU. In Britain BHA affiliated to the United Nations Association and supported Freedom from Hunger and similar campaigns (with special insistence on the need for population control). They also helped with projects such as the first non-racial co-educational secondary school in Bechuanaland and ways of raising rural standards in Bihar.

At home, BHA was involved with setting up the Humanist Housing Association, the Agnostics Adoption Society and a counselling service to help people with personal problems. The early work shows the great interest shown in alleviating human problems, as BHA continued and strengthened to today's far-reaching and influential programme of activities.

Education continues to be a priority and many books, newsletters and literature have been produced. *Humanity*, the bi-monthly newsletter, was replaced by *Humanist News* when *New Humanist* (RPA) was issued to BHA members from 2001. Also in 2001 came the suggestion of the name change to the Humanist Society of England and Wales, to correspond with the Scottish and Northern Ireland counterparts.

(BHA registered charity no: 285987 details see Contacts on page 93.)

What I believe

Throughout his writing, E.M. Forster portrayed his humanist interests, not as a Humanist in the early days of the twentieth century, but as an agnostic. By speaking through his characters he was able to express his own humanistic views: 'He cared for the universe, for the tiny tangle in it that we call civilisation, for his fellow men who made the tangle and who transcended it. Love, the love of humanity, warmed him. . .'

His path to agnosticism, and ultimately Humanism, is described in his inaugural presidential address given at an annual meeting of Cambridge Humanists. Having had a conventionally religious childhood, with unenthusiastic religious interest at school, he moved on to Cambridge where his Christianity 'quietly and quickly disappeared'. He began to question, at first the Trinity which he found *very odd*. 'I tried to defend it in accordance with my inherited tenets, but it kept falling apart like an unmanageable toy.' Having discarded this aspect of his religious belief he realised he had jeopardised the stability of the rest, so he started to think more deeply about that too, and his rejection was complete.

From 1946 E.M. Forster was a leading member of Cambridge Humanists, and became its president in 1959. He was a member of the Ethical Union in the 1950s and on the Advisory Council of BHA in the 60s. His particular interest was in broadcasting, and he often defended Humanism in the press and on radio. Through his articles he examined his attitudes to major issues and, in setting out his belief in personal relationships, he saw them as a way of giving order to 'contemporary chaos'. He decried power that corrupts and the loss of individual freedom.

Under the title, *What I Believe*, BHA put together three of Forster's articles, together with a useful introduction by Nicolas Walter with brief biographical details. Together, the articles form a comprehensive view of Humanism. The writing flows with such ease that it has an up-to-date feel, and it is hard to realise that the articles are taken from collections first published between 1938 and 1972. E.M.Forster wrote at a time when Faith was the 'norm', so to express his disbelief could have jeopardised his position had he not already been accepted as one of Britain's eminent writers.

(*What I Believe by E.M.Forster see Bibliography on page 92.*)

Charity begins anywhere

I had a neighbour who regularly turned out her cupboards. Each Christmas her son's toys were culled to make room for new ones, even though the 'old' were still in virtually new condition. Her dustbin overflowed. And I was horrified, because she genuinely believed that no one else would want her family's 'cast offs', as she called them. But just as every grain of sand makes a beach, so too does every unwanted item make a charity shop!

The first charity shop was opened by Oxfam in 1948. Other charities' shops began to blossom over the last thirty or forty years and all proved to be an excellent way of raising money at grass roots level. The new and the older established — British Red Cross, Save the Children, Age Concern, Oxfam, to name a few — are all out there doing valuable work. They have the organisational infrastructure to get the most out of the help provided and money raised. But whatever the organisation, and in whatever capacity its helpers are working, it is individuals who come together for a few hours, a few days or all their spare time.

Many people say, 'What do Humanists do?' The answer is a great deal. But helping existing charities seldom hits the headlines. Yet, where an organisation exists for a particular need, it would be a diminishing of resources to set up another as a specifically *Humanist* charity. Help is help wherever it comes from.

Charity, and the acts of ultimate organisation that follow, starts by one individual having an idea, discussing it and helping to put that idea into action. One individual discussed with his wife the possibility of dividing a house into flats for elderly people, and from it grew the Humanist Housing Association (see pages 85-6). One Humanist nurse set in motion a successful campaign to stop the closure of a hospital radiotherapy machine. Another started the initiative to raise money to send nurses to Africa. Raising money to help deprived rural communities in India was the idea of another Humanist.

Countless more see a need and act upon it — in the same way that countless others with different life-stances give help where it is needed. Charity should not be categorised under organisational headings, inferring that only certain members of the community think of others. Charity is an attitude of mind.

Laughter,
the counterbalance

Sometimes Humanists and Rationalists
are accused of being too serious, always
finding a *reason* and often philosophising
rather than seeing the humorous side of things.
Yet laughter has for many years been recognised
as therapeutic. So much so that in the early 1990s the West
Birmingham Health Authority set up an NHS Laughter Clinic, with
themes that included 'happy thinking', 'achieving an inner smile'
and 'releasing the joy of the inner fun child'. And in India there are
600 similar laughter clubs.

an incongruity

But laughter can come at any time, whether with people or not;
listening to the radio or reading a book — at any odd moment of
incongruity which gives an unexpected conflict or inconsistency
between two ideas.

Television and printed media can show us a world of unhappiness and cruelty. Whether tensions are greater today, or
whether people are less able to cope, is open to discussion.
Whatever the reason, frustrations build up. And the act of laughing,
like yawning, sneezing and crying, relieves tension.

Finding the funny angle doesn't have to be frivolous, it just
makes us human. Of course there are times when this isn't possible
or appropriate, but like all serious situations they need their
counterbalance. Recognising the 'incongruity', whether verbal or
visual causes the smile that often turns to laughter.

Smiling relaxes innumerable muscles in the face; laughter goes
further, expanding the lungs, relaxing shoulder muscles and adding
a 'lift' to the whole body. But Plato described humour as
malevolent, and later philosophers equated humour with ignorance
and foolishness. Fortunately, modern psychologists regard humour,
and the laughter that goes with it, as beneficial, even essential.
Freud saw laughter as a means of safely discharging nervous
energy. More recent research emphasises the clinical and social
value of creating laughter.

Whatever the reason, whatever the cause, laughter, genuine
laughter, is certainly good for us.

Humanism in America

The American Humanist Association (AHA), founded in 1941 as a nonprofit-making, educational organisation, organises and supports local Humanist chapters (groups) in major American cities. AHA has an active outreach programme that provides Humanist celebrants, advocates, speakers and advisers to help those needing non-sectarian assistance from a naturalistic, philosophical viewpoint. The *Humanist* is the monthly journal of AHA, and *Free Mind* the bi-monthly newsletter. Under 'Humanist Press Books', AHA publishes titles on Humanist philosophy.

The Council for Secular Humanism (CSH) also a nonprofit-making, tax-exempt, educational organisation, is housed at the Center for Inquiry, which is an international centre of secular humanism and free thought. Its libraries, conference and seminar facilities are used by secularists worldwide.

(AHA: www.humanist.net CSH: www.secularhumanism.org)

* * * * *

Humanism in Canada

By the 1950s and 60s Humanist groups across Canada were particularly strong in Toronto, Montreal, Vancouver and Victoria. In 1968, Dr Henry Morgentaler, who was president of the Humanist Fellowship of Montreal, helped found the Humanist Association of Canada (HAC) and became its first president. Lloyd Brereton, also a founding member, had started a local humanist magazine in Victoria, and with the emergence of HAC produced the national magazine, *Humanist in Canada*.

Humanists in Montreal worked towards abortion law reform which resulted in the 'Morgentaler amendment', whereby higher courts could no longer reverse a jury's finding of 'not guilty'. Across Canada, Humanists provide non-religious funerals and counselling, and HAC has always played a strong role in lobbying support for many social causes. According to *Statistics Canada*, three million people in Canada have no religious belief and, as knowledge increases of how the Earth has evolved, many are looking for something to take over the role that religion once had.

(Details: www. magi.com/~hac/)

Encourage young scepticism

I used to try very hard to be a believer. I wanted to believe there was a tooth fairy, that Father Christmas really was a down-the-chimney mystery, that there were fairies at the bottom of the garden and that adults told the truth, but I never managed it.

I must have been a tiresome child with whom to deal, because I argued so much. I'm told I perfected the extremely infuriating use of the word 'why' before I learnt to say 'shan't!' and I have a vivid memory of being stingingly smacked at infant school because, when a teacher told me that 'Jesus would cry if I was naughty', I asked how he would know. And when she told me it was because he watched all of us all the time, I remarked that he must be very rude if he watched people in the lavatory, and anyway I'd see him watching me if he did and kick him for it. (That was what we'd been told to do if any of the little boys in our playground came spying on us in the lavs. I thought she'd understand that. But she didn't. . .)

I rather think the belief business finally bit the dust for me after that experience at age five. I was labelled as a troublemaker from then on. Because the walloping made me so angry, I told her there wasn't any Jesus anyway and she'd made it all up just like they'd made it up about Father Christmas. I don't for a moment think I was an unusual child. I think the majority of children are natural sceptics. Watch them watching conjurers and you'll see the brightest of them trying to look under the silk scarf and boxes and other tricksy bits to see how it's done. It takes a very deft magician indeed to really fool children; that's why the successful ones are those who make jokes and allow the children to laugh. They forgive the pretence of magic in exchange for the fun.

The trouble is that all these children go on to be bullied into irrational belief. It used to amaze me, as I got older and reached the level of school where they taught us physics and chemistry, that the selfsame teachers who taught us the rules of scientific evidence, of the way experiments had to be repeatable to be true, of the way mathematics provided incontrovertible evidence of so many laws of nature, could stand in daily school prayers with their hands folded and eyes closed praying to a supernatural totally unproven being. Weird or what? Even weirder was the way they too were enraged and punitive if a pupil said that Darwin had proved the bible was nonsense.

The thing I found most difficult, I have to say, was feeling such an outsider. All the other people in my form were believers, swallowing grown-up duplicity in large lumps, reading newspaper horoscopes eagerly, telling fortunes with tarot cards and such like, and it was lonely thinking differently. So I used to pretend to believe in the same things they did, until a Walt Whitman poem, encountered in an English class this time rather than good old science, brought me up short again. In *Song of Myself* he says: 'I think I could turn and live with animals. They are so placid and self-contained. They do not bow down and worship one of their own kind. . .'

That one really did get to me. It not only confirmed my disbelief in supernatural gods (what was Jesus but a man, after all?) it also made me a republican. But that's another story. Anyway, after that poem came into my life, I stopped trying to be the White Queen who could, Lewis Carroll said, believe six impossible things before breakfast, and settled for the form outsider. It might be lonely, but it wasn't too bad. After all, Walt Whitman sort of agreed with me.

As time went on, and I left school behind me to get a real education, borrowing the likes of Thomas Paine, John Locke and Thomas Hobbes, I at last discovered that there were real live people and not just dead poets and philosophers who thought like me, and that I wasn't a weirdo after all. From then on, the struggle to be a believer disappeared into the other horrors of childhood memories, there to cease to be of any trouble at all. I was a real live grown up at last and refusal to share others' illusions/delusions no longer marked me out as weird at best, despicable at worst. *CR*

(Claire Rayner's contribution for RPA's centenary issue of New Humanist.)

* * * * *

Who's for Humanism?

For some time, a friend wondered why coastal resorts bordering East and West Sussex had so much interest in Humanism. Everywhere he went, BHA was graffitied on the walls in large letters. It was only later that an ardent football fan explained that the letters stood for Brighton and Hove Albion!

Environmentally thinking

Global warming, that once crept into our consciousness, has now jumped to the fore. Changing weather patterns are producing floods, tornadoes, droughts and extremes of temperature throughout the world. And it is widely reported that humans are responsible because of causing holes in the ozone layer.

At the same time, the concentrated production of food, creating 'mountains' in one area and starvation in another, has added to environmental changes that exacerbate disasters as well as resulting in agricultural practices which are causing alarm.

In the early nineteen-sixties, an American zoologist, Rachel Carson, wrote of the danger to us and the environment through over-use of chemicals. Her book, *Silent Spring,* not only stirred American conscience, but the effects rippled outwards to become a major reference point and an influence on later understanding of environmental issues. 'Rachel Carson uncovered the hiding places of facts that should have been disclosed to the public long before,' said Frank Graham in *Since Silent Spring.*

As a writer, Rachel Carson was eminently suited to exposing the problems because of her duel interest in the diversity of living things and her scientific research which led her to study genetics and marine biology, resulting in a master's degree and subsequent experience in both fields. But *Silent Spring* had a divided reception because of the impact it would have on the agri-chemical industry. Yet, the warnings it raised and the questions it posed remain just as valid today.

At that time it was thought by many that eradicating pests in the soil and on plants could only be beneficial to humans. But pests developed an immunity, so stronger chemicals were needed. What was not considered, again by many, was that small insects are eaten by birds or small animals that are eaten by larger animals, and humans are often at the end of the food chain that is affected. It was also not appreciated that non-biodegradable chemicals are stored in fat tissue, thus accumulating through the chain.

When birds died, it was later conceded, they were not seen as 'sensitive and responsive indices to the health and quality of the total environment, of which man is a part.' Each localised incident was viewed as just that, *a localised incident*, and not placed in context with other environmental incidents throughout the world. Most of our actions affect other people and the environment, but because the effects are often postponed, the long term results are in many cases not seen.

The aim of *Silent Spring* was to bring together many strands of the same problem, and not just to show the environmental and health problems being caused, but to offer effective biologically controlled alternatives to the over-use of chemicals. Rachel Carson could not have foreseen the diverse environmental problems that would arise, but she sounded a warning that was only partially heeded. Since publication of her book, environmental issues in all spheres began to be taken more seriously. Although it was a slow process, change in attitude resulted. The altering weather conditions, that immediately affect people, accelerated that change by showing how urgent the need is to respect the interrelationship between all living things.

Animal species have always affected the environment, but to a lesser extent compared with humans, either by over-grazing or damaging the habitat. The difference today is that we are capable of far greater destruction, yet at the same time we have the ability to know what we are doing. Maybe at last we are trying to do something about it.

(Silent Spring and Since Silent Spring see Bibliography on page 92.)

* * * * *

Potted profile — 2

Gene Roddenberry, a leading member of the American Humanist Association (AHA), created *Star Trek*, although Spock, Kirk and 'Beam me up Scotty!' are better known than their creator. He was born in El Paso, Texas, in 1921, and became an atheist in his teens. Later he discovered that Humanism encapsulated his rational, compassionate philosophy which greatly influenced his writing and the production of *Star Trek*. Co-operation and mutual encouragement, peaceful problem solving, equal dignity and respect for life forms, no dogma or doctrine, reliance on science to find facts, and enjoyment of emotions and intuitions are all basic to the scripts. He said that *Star Trek* was his statement to the world, not just his political philosophy but his overview of life and the human condition. Gene Roddenberry died in 1991, five months after receiving the AHA Humanist Arts Award.

Humanism in schools

Teenagers — those mysterious, turbulent, aggressive and troubled human beings, spend most of their waking hours at school. School is sometimes perceived as a secure island in a sea of uncertainty and suspicion. School is a place where an adolescent girl, eyes swollen with tears and sobbing with distress after some hurtful incident at home, can rush into the waiting and comforting arms of her friends. A young footballer can hardly wait to tell his mates at school all about the two goals he scored at the weekend for the local youth team. But school, that microcosm of the real world, has a darker side — the boy who refuses to go, dreading the bully waiting for him; the girl terrified of the gym changing room; the sensitive boy made miserable by taunts of 'gay'.

Schools have long recognised that they have a responsibility for far more than the delivery of an academic curriculum. Like it or not, they have assumed the role of social worker, police force, counsellor and parent. Most students in school know that they rely on other people: peers, teaching staff, caretakers, technicians — any sympathetic person to help when things go wrong.

All schools are required to implement a programme of 'ethical, moral, spiritual education' — call it what you will. The Government is also anxious to add some form of 'civics' and political knowledge. With the continuing commitment to religious education, the overcrowded curriculum begins to burst at the seams. The efforts of various governments to push even harder to promote numeracy, literacy, science and technology leave little space in the curriculum for the study of history, geography, art, drama and literature — the traditional framework of the humanities. Many schools attempted to remove the barriers between these subjects under a broad programme of 'Humanities'. In this way, a study of Ancient Egypt would show the geographical conditions leading to settlement of areas, the historical development of the state and the religious structure which bound the whole together.

Teenagers have a real empathy with the culture and problems of their own and other societies. The squeezing of the Humanities is a serious threat to this need. Governments find this difficult to understand and still insist on some form of religious and moral pressure to subdue teenage rebellion and anti-social behaviour.

School students prefer to put their trust in the support of other people rather than expect help from the supernatural. The Humanist ideal of faith in humanity would find a ready response from most young people at school.

Traditionally, schools have relied on an assembly as a focus for stability, responsibility and the finer things in life. Ask most students what they think about assembly and you are likely to receive a pretty negative assessment. Teachers will give a very similar response. The days are long gone when the headteacher can get away with a hymn and a prayer. And just try getting teachers to take an assembly. And yet ... and yet ... the whole school gathers together to start the day in companionship, the sense of belonging, the sharing of good news and bad, the celebration of success, the sharing of sorrow and the dissemination of information. Some schools even announce birthdays, news about pets and offer articles for sale.

This part of an assembly is always enjoyed, but when you get to the moral, ethical or religious bit, it's a very different story. The thing students loathe is being 'preached at'. They respond to an approach that engages their sympathy and support. National and international news items, local issues, appeals for help, charitable activities, local youth programmes, sport (national and local), usually receive a sympathetic response. Children at school are interested in other human beings and will be attracted by the human experience.

Historically, schools have recognised a 'hidden curriculum', a strategy for including a vein of altruism into the normal content of lessons. The Humanist ideal fits naturally into this design. It would be odd if a lesson on Ancient Greece failed to leave a student with the impression that Athens was a much more liberating and exciting place than Sparta. A series of experiments to determine methods of generating cheap energy will be given added relevance if related to the needs of the impoverished and energy-starved Third World.

Denominational religious instruction has no place in schools. How can the problems of Northern Ireland be solved when some children attend Protestant schools and others go to Catholic schools? Children should not be divided by religion, but appreciate one another as human beings. Isn't that what Humanism is all about? *BSt*

Unweaving rainbows

It has sometimes been argued that a knowledge of science diminishes our appreciation of life. But when Newton used a prism to create an artificial rainbow, it did not lesson the beauty of the colours revealed from white light — it magnified their beauty with the added knowledge of how those colours were created.

When Richard Dawkins was accused of giving a 'cold bleak message' in his analytical scientific approach to life he said:

> To accuse science of robbing life of the warmth that makes it worth living is so preposterously mistaken, so diametrically opposite to my own feelings and those of most working scientists, that I am almost driven to the despair of which I am wrongly suspected.

The wonder of science and the poetry of science, he believed, must be missing in those who think it a sterile, mechanical subject. To help unfold this wonder and poetry, Richard Dawkins wrote *Unweaving the Rainbow*, a book that makes you appreciate that, whatever your lot in life, it is a 'miracle' that you were born. And having been one of the lucky few that have come through the millions of odds against being born, we should open our eyes to the wonders around us. A theme of often-perceived conflict between poetry and science runs through the book, yet Richard Dawkins sees no conflict.

By validating the wonder of science, he shows us that being jolted from our 'anaesthetic of familiarity' we can appreciate the way that unweaving rainbows adds to the poetry of science. Other themes flowing through the book reveal the diversity and wonder of scientific influence on our lives. Understanding why cuckoos' eggs have developed so that they are not rejected by the host bird in no way detracts from the wonder of their acceptance:

> Whether in the analysis of starlight or sound waves, animal footprints or human DNA, the seemingly miraculous world that science continues to reveal should inspire rather than undermine the poetic imagination.

Far from diminishing the poetry of life, Richard Dawkins shows that unweaving rainbows immeasurably adds to it.

(Unweaving the Rainbow by Richard Dawkins see Bibliography page 92.)

Leonardo — *1452-1519*

In one of Leonardo da Vinci's copiousnote books he wrote, 'We should not desire the impossible.' But his thirst for knowledge, which remained with him all his life, carried him to its threshold.

At first without training, he began drawing as a young boy, and studied and drew all kinds of creatures and plants he collected from his garden in Vinci. Dissecting them to examine their make-up, he learnt not only to draw in detail but how each one was designed. This awareness helped him later with his intricately designed inventions.

Leonardo's father wanted him to join the family business as a lawyer, not believing he could become an artist. It was only when one of Leonardo's paintings was shown to Verrocchio, in Florence, that the father agreed to allow his son, at sixteen, to be apprenticed to the great painter. As an artist, light, shadows and reflections were important to Leonardo, but his interest went way beyond drawing and painting.

His desire for knowledge covered music, architecture, anatomy, geometry, aviation, hydrology and military fortifications. Because of his dedication to what he called 'the inner adventure', he concentrated his time on vast programmes of discovery and invention, with results only 'invented' many years later. By watching birds flying, he drew the movement of their wings, noting the aerodynamics of flight which led him to draw 'flying machines' beyond his time. And his interest in anatomy showed him how people moved, thus he designed machines for many different jobs. He also discovered how the eye's lens is controlled by muscles for distance sight or bright light.

For three hundred years Leonardo's notebooks were not found. Written in mirror writing, they showed drawings and plans for submarines, aircraft, parachutes, a girder bridge — the same construction as the Bailey Bridge first used in the Second World War. Convinced that overcrowding and contaminated water caused the Black Plague to spread through Milan, he devised a system of underground piped water. But his ideas were too strange or too new to be accepted. The principles, however, later proved sound.

Background to the —

International Humanist and Ethical Union

IHEU is the only umbrella organisation of Humanist, rationalist, atheist, secularist, ethical culture and agnostic groups around the world. Its member organisations range from large membership groups to specialist bodies such as publishers, universities and development agencies. There are also individual supporters. Until 1952, the body of Humanist thought developed as independent national organisations, but a need was felt for a voice to represent them all on a worldwide basis. And so IHEU came into being:

> The Ethical Union [UK], after some exploration with some surviving elements of the World Union of Freethinkers, took the initiative with the Dutch Humanist League in calling a congress in Amsterdam in 1952 which inaugurated the International Humanist and Ethical Union. Sir Julian Huxley presided over the congress, and the founding members were the Dutch Humanist League, The Belgian Humanist League, The British Ethical Union, the American Ethical Union, the American Humanist Association and the Indian Radical Humanist Movement. *Harold Blackham, Humanism*

There are over three million members in over thirty countries including Nepal, Peru, Iceland, Ghana, Russia ... (see pages 24, 44, 63, 83). Funded by donations and membership dues from member organisations and individual supporters, IHEU is democratically run. The headquarters is in London, but regional and specialist secretariats and networks are organised in many different countries. It is strongly committed to the ideals of the UN and the first directors of UNESCO (Julian Huxley), FAO (John Boyd Orr) and WHO (G. Brock Chisholm) were prominent Humanists. Many humanist principles, and the humanist attitude, form the philosophical basis of the concept of human rights as stated in the *Universal Declaration of Human Rights.*

IHEU has participated in the FAO's five-year Freedom From Hunger Campaign, is a founding member of the UNESCO NGO Working Group on Science and Ethics and is represented at major UN conferences. Outside the UN, IHEU and its member organisations have defended civil liberties, promoted more humane and rational attitudes to abortion law, sexual relationships, voluntary euthanasia, capital punishment, criminal reformation and the exploitation of animals.

Together with its Dutch specialist member, HIVOS, IHEU funds member organisation activities in the third world through the *Humanist Networking and Development Programme*. This includes community development, literacy and good citizenship, a Humanist school in India, Humanist groups in Africa, promoting the scientific outlook, Humanist books (Chinese, Hindi) and magazines (Spanish, Mexican), examining the religious abuse of children and help with the legal fight against blasphemy laws.

Practical activities in the community by organised Humanists are as diverse as the defence of democracy, protection of civil rights, provision of sheltered housing for the elderly and helping victims of religious and sexual intolerance and persecution. The International Humanist and Ethical Youth Organisation (IHEYO) caters for ages from 18 to 30 with a website for discussion groups, directory of worldwide members and youth organisations.

Humanist organisations in many countries provide social and personal support through education, counselling and community care, where hundreds of Humanist professional moral educators and counsellors are employed in schools, hospitals, prisons and the armed forces. Humanist groups in Asia work for democracy, women's emancipation and eradication of harmful superstition, while Humanists in Canada and Europe have fought for contraception and abortion rights. Many Humanist groups offer non-religious rites of passage (naming ceremonies, weddings, funerals). Still more fight for the separation of religion and state, promote the scientific attitude and campaign against the genital mutilation of female children in Islamic societies.

To achieve their goals, Humanist groups also publish literature, contribute articles to newspapers, radio and TV, create websites, organise seminars, workshops and conferences. And IHEU produces the quarterly *International Humanist News*. The fourteenth Congress, which was held in India in 1999, had the theme *Humanism for Human Development and Happiness*. The following year Congress was in Melbourne, with the theme *Ethics and Values for the Next Century*. July 2002 marks IHEU's 50th anniversary, with Congress in the Netherlands with the theme, *Living together locally and globally*.

(See Contacts on page 93.)

Listening — earthquake in Hazelmere

Two patients recovering in hospital sat and chatted together. They appeared engrossed in their conversation as the chatter went back and forth in a pleasant, animated way. It was only as I neared them that I realised they were relaying, in turn, the details of their operations and what their doctors had told them. They both made the cursory 'Oh, did he?' and 'You poor soul', before continuing with 'Now my doctor said. . .'

The patients weren't actually listening to what was being said, but they were using each other as a *listening post*; an excuse to talk and someone to talk *at* while they came to terms with their own situation. It was their need for someone to be there, ostensibly to listen, that made their 'conversation' mutually beneficial.

At the other extreme, a personnel manager said that after individual employees had come to see him to discuss their problems, they thanked him for his help and said how much better they felt after being able to talk things over. But the personnel manager had said very little as he allowed the other to talk. Having an understanding *listener* was all the employees needed.

Everyday conversation is seldom as intense as the patients' or as one-sided as the employees'. But there are times when, while one person is talking another is concentrating so hard on what he or she wants to say that s/he does not engage or respond at all. In our eagerness to make our point we simply mumble 'Mmm' or 'I see' until we can get our chance to speak.

The TV series, *Yes, Prime Minister*, gave a good example of how bad we are at listening. The Prime Minister continued sorting papers saying, 'Yes.' 'I see.' 'Right.' while Sir Humphrey was giving the day's schedule. To see what the reaction would be, Sir Humphrey added, 'And there was an earthquake in Hazelmere.' 'Good,' said the Prime Minister, in the same matter of fact way.

Maybe we all switch off at times when someone goes on and on. But I admired the person who listened to every minute detail when another spent a quarter of an hour explaining how he rewired an iron! To be a good listener is more than a valuable asset, it is an essential need in today's often frenetic world. And listening requires an interest not only in what is being said, but in the person saying it.

Why I'm a Humanist — 2

As a young child, my family and teachers told me that I was Church of England. I accepted this, assuming that with their greater experience they must know best. I remember, however, being increasingly puzzled at being expected to believe tales of miracles and resurrection in religion, whilst being encouraged to think for myself in other subjects such as science and literature.

As a teenager I became sceptical of how an all-powerful god would allow the cruelty and injustice I saw in the world. In 1954, I remember being impressed by Margaret Knight's article in the Listener, 'Morals Without Religion', which we read in the sixth form at school. Most of my fellow students fell in line with general public criticism of these views, and regretfully I did not have the courage to stand out and admit that I thought her ideas sounded very sensible. In those days I wanted to conform.

I thought it seemed sensible that morals should be based on human instincts and experience, rather than on acceptance of dogmas and superstitions somehow attributed to a mysterious supernatural power. Also, conflicts between the different dogmas of different religions seemed to be contributing to much unrest in the world.

It was studying geology at university that really convinced me that I could not accept Christianity. I discovered at first hand the wonders of evolution in the fossil record and came to an awareness of the vast natural changes and timescale of earth's history. The bible's account of early life seemed unrealistic.

For some years I then loosely thought of myself as an agnostic, but, like many young people, I pushed serious thoughts of religion and philosophy into the background to concentrate on the practicalities of career and family life. It was as I approached retirement, with more time to pause and reflect, that I felt an urge to look more closely into Humanism and express my concerns about continuing religious privileges and discrimination in society — indoctrination of worship in schools; prayers at public ceremonies; an established church with special privileges.

I have now reached a firm conviction that Humanism, and not religion, presents a logical framework for our approach to the future of mankind. *RM*

If music be. . .

It is not the origins of music but the content — its beat, melody, rhythm, change of key and counterpoint — that are appreciated when music is experienced. Going back thousands of years to war-cries, chanting, hunting, harvest and victory 'songs', it can be seen how these expressions released feelings of joy, sadness, anger, courage or pride. Through banging, stamping, clapping and chanting, music grew, until simple instruments began to be created. But all the while *feelings* were being expressed.

Greek vases, Egyptian carvings, pictures and embroideries of China and India show some of these early musical instruments and this need for musical expression. Many years later religious music had the same function, when it was commissioned by wealthy patrons to be written by struggling musicians, who were happy to have this patronage in order to compose. Much music was religious in origin by tradition, because religion permeated all society. It was also a crime to profess disbelief.

In the last 1,000 years, the church has played the key role in the creation of music. From the earliest plainchant to Bach's St Matthew Passion, landmarks in the art form have been occurring within church walls: the first notated music, Gregorian chant, the flowering of polyphony, the triumph of counterpoint in the works of Vivaldi, Bach and Handel. Whether or not such composers were simply doing a job, or whether it was a spiritual vocation, in many cases we shall never know. *BBC Music Magazine December '99*

But running in parallel with early sacred music had been the popular musicians, strolling fiddlers and singers who primarily improvised, with no desire or ability to commit their tunes to paper. This was the music of the people, putting into song frustrations and happenings around them, in the same way that today's pop music reflects the feelings of the composers.

When Paul Macartney sang *Amazing Grace* and Cat Stevens *Morning Has Broken*, the settings, not words, popularised them. And just as today we may enjoy the tune, though not necessarily agreeing with, understanding or even *hearing* the words, so too were the old folk songs and religious songs often appreciated.

Humanism is about life, and music as an intricate part of it rises

37

above controversy. Julian Huxley said: 'Beethoven's posthumous quartets can transport us to another world, make us free of another realm of being.'* It is the beauty of the music and the ability to transcend its original purpose that is the test of a great work, and helps us to override our technological age:

> A wide-ranging Humanism will always seek to extend to more and more people, through education and opportunity, the enrichment of the personality which music gives. In our technological society we should be warned by Darwin: 'The loss of these tastes (for one or more of the arts according to our predilections) is a loss of happiness and may possibly be injurious to the intellect and more probably to the moral character, by enfeebling the emotional part of our nature.'
> *Michael Tippett**

Our appreciation of, and need for, music, whatever its origins, is fundamental to humanity, for it is the harmonious effect, relaxing or stirring qualities that enrich us.

(Quotations from The Humanist Frame see Bibliography on page 93.)

* * * * *

Chance and choice

After standing up in church to disagree with the sermon, Brenden Butler rationalised his own ideas in a monograph called *A Concept of Creation: the chance and choice theory*. In this brief extract he shows how life is affected by both chance and choice:

'Mankind's actions and thoughts can affect the choice factor, but only where nature's laws are not compromised. Nothing is set on an unalterable course, with the universe grinding away to an inevitable end. The chance/choice theory shows that evil and suffering, wars and natural disasters are a product of natural laws and human intervention created by human consciousness. This logical balance is part of the wonderful concept of creation that we are caught up in and with which we are inextricably entwined.

Everything is borrowed, however temporarily, in a journey to and from the environment. We need to understand this in order to have a proper sense of our role and responsibility, and to feel the indebtedness we should show and our need to pay back what we have received. We must become the caretakers rather than the controllers of creation, and we can do this best if we truly appreciate the wonders of it.' *BB*

Network of families

"Where are all the young ones?" was the cry that began the Humanist Family Network in 1995.

Humanist events did not cater for children, and adults with younger families could rarely spare time to attend. We needed family-centred opportunities to meet and socialise, and to share the experiences of bringing up children or growing up within a school system — indeed a society — that still assumes religious belief. We wanted adults and children to enjoy being Humanists together, in a relaxed way, and as a matter of course.

The Network has grown up around an annual weekend at a venue which accommodates us all but is small enough to give us exclusive use. In practice, this has meant youth hostels, which nowadays are surprisingly comfortable. We avoid regimentation, but regular features have evolved. There is a talk and discussion around a family-centred theme, a children's event and the opportunity to join one of several groups heading for local attractions. An optional extra night extends the event for those who wish it.

We try to see that all who want to be are involved, and there is much doubling up of transport, 'swapping' of children between families and catching up from previous years. Friendships have developed between families, and many keep in touch and meet between annual weekends. We welcome newcomers, and we encourage grandparents to bring grandchildren. A regular sprinkling of overseas visitors has brought us different perspectives. One of the most gratifying aspects has been children's eager anticipation of the annual weekend.

We keep the Network under review: Are there affordable alternatives to youth hostels? Could we include more options and if so what? How do we cater for older children as the 'regulars' move into their teens? Is there scope for more than one event a year? The planning is largely in the hands of the Network members, with the organisation provided by BHA as a membership service. Although the Network is intended for BHA members, we welcome first-time families at the weekend who are sympathetic to our views and simply want to try meeting and mixing with Humanists. *RP*

Over-population can't go on

✳ Since 1900 world population has more than quadrupled.
✳ It has now reached the six billion mark.
✳ Our planet cannot sustain this incredible growth rate.

Not only are resources in danger of running out, but disposing of waste is causing increasing problems. We are also helping to destroy the habitats of other species, which in turn adversely affects all life. Even so, partly due to the success of family planning, Europe has undergone a demographic transition by moving from high birth and death rates to our present low birth and death rates, with stable or declining population.

Surprisingly, the idea of family planning was put forward by Jeremy Bentham, in 1797, and Francis Place, a Radical, tried to popularise it in the early 19th century. In 1832, *The Fruits of Philosophy or the Private Companion of Young Married People* was published in America. But when a Bristol bookseller was later prosecuted for selling it, Annie Besant and Charles Bradlaugh published the book in London to provoke a test case. Their sentences were quashed on appeal, but the publicity helped book sales. Yet, it wasn't until Marie Stopes opened a clinic in 1921 that family planning became more acceptable in the UK. Other clinics followed and in 1930 formed the Family Planning Association.

The greatest worry today is that many poorer countries object to birth control for religious or cultural reasons, which exacerbates the spiralling problem of over-population and declining resources. This affects not just their own country but the whole world. Writing in *Rationalism for the Twenty-First Century*, Diane Brown, co-founder of the World Population Foundation in the Netherlands, said:

> Governments can, without coercion, create a climate of opinion where spacing of births and limitations in family size are seen as desirable — despite religious opposition. Major factors in reducing fertility are: raising the status of women, education (particularly for women and girls), primary health care and access to reproductive health care, including family planning. ... Population growth is a solvable problem, but it requires attention, commitment and resources.

(Rationalism for the Twenty-First Century see Bibliography on page 92.)

Early philosophy: humanist thought

Epicurus

By the 6th century BCE, a group of Ionian Greeks, who lived on the coast of Asia Minor, started to investigate the nature of the universe. They were in contact with Mesopotamian civilisations and learned from the Babylonian traditions of astronomy, mathematics and science. But their interest went beyond observing and recording. They began looking for natural explanations for the world around them, and so became the first philosophers and 'intellectuals'.

Water, air and indestructible matter were in turn each seen as the basic, primary substance of the universe. But **Heraclitus** of Ephesus (c540-480BCE) saw the universe as being in a state of continual change. He is reputed to have taught that one cannot step into the same river twice because no flowing river is ever the same. He saw a dynamic tension between opposites governed by natural laws which human reason could determine.

In seeking reasons, early philosophers no longer relied on myths and handed-down stories, which before had provided answers. 'They reached their conclusions through observation and rational thought in which religion and gods played no direct role. By the 6th century BCE, much of Greek society was ready to tolerate such non-religious, rational teaching.' (*Kishlansky*)

Interest spread, and many discussions took place with Athenians and others drawn to the city. They examined the past and present and started to question traditional values. Some philosophers studied the powers and limitations of the human mind. Others, such as **Protagoras** (c490-421BCE), examined the complexity of human reason.

It is surprising to think that **Democritus** (c450-370BCE) put forward the theory of the world being composed of atoms. He said knowledge is based on experience through the senses and that ethics and behaviour stem from the natural, not a supernatural, world. Democritus has been called the *prince of philosophers* and a great investigator of nature. **Epicurus** (341-270BCE) was greatly influenced by Democritus and further developed his teaching that the natural world is not designed by a supernatural power. In

41

Athens, Epicurus established a philosophical school in a tranquil garden community of peace and freedom from fear. This became a model for other Epicurean schools, and widely accepted over the 600 years of early Greek and Roman civilisation.

Later, **Lucretius** (100-55BCE), a Roman poet, continued to develop these ideas. His epic poem *De Rerum Natura* (On the Nature of the Universe) popularised the philosophical theories of Democritus and Epicurus, and denounced religious beliefs which Lucretius saw as one of the greatest sources of fear and misery. The poem follows an account of the immense period of time during which the sun, moon and stars appeared without design. Then following a natural progression came plants, animals and human beings.

Another Roman orator, **Cicero** (106-43BCE), adopted the Greek model of education based on a study of the great poets, historians and philosophers. It was known as *humanitas,* meaning humane conduct, and was later developed by Renaissance scholars, who were called 'humanists' because they tried to cultivate an open mind. As knowledge and experience grew, freethinkers/humanists developed a more rational approach to life which was not bound by religious dogma. They questioned assumptions that had long been accepted. Yet they always appreciated the beauty and vastness of the universe. Today, continually expanding knowledge puts our own lives into this perspective.

* * * * *

Potted profile — 3

Richard Leakey was born in Kenya in 1944. From an early age, his archaeologist and anthropologist parents, Louis and Mary, taught him 'bushcraft' and how to recognise fossils. Because of his interest and practical experience he became a palaeo-anthropologist. Having learnt to fly, he noted from the air what was to become an important site of fossilised hominoid bones. His books and television series, *The Making of Mankind* and *Human Origins*, made anthropology accessible to the wider public. He became the director of the National Museum of Kenya in 1974 and is now a leading advocate for the conservation of wild animals and their habitat. In summing up human consciousness he said, 'We should rejoice at so wondrous a product of evolution.'

(See Bibliography on page 92 for books by Richard Leakey.)

All in the mind

While Ludovic Kennedy was in Newfoundland during his wartime naval service someone lent him a copy of Thomas Paine's *The Rights of Man*. This started him reading works of other radical authors. His book, *All in the Mind*, outlines his thoughts and beliefs, summarising many of the ideas of writers he has come across. He came to reject organised religion finding it based on myths and superstitions, and so became an atheist.

The reader is taken through the development of the early Christian church, and continues through the centuries to today. The section on early atheists describes the 16th century French churchman who, at the age of 60, published a book *Concerning Wisdom* recanting his beliefs. This quotation seems relevant over 400 years later: 'All religions, without exception, share the same characteristics. All discover and publicise miracles, prodigies, oracles, sacred mysteries, saints, prophets, festivals, articles of faith and beliefs necessary for salvation; each pretends to be better and truer than the others. . .' Ludovic Kennedy explains his own 'spiritual' fulfilment through art and nature. *PA*

I enjoyed reading *All in the Mind*, partly because it closely reflects my own view on religion, but also because it is easily readable and clearly conveys the deep personal feelings of the author. The book questions the way God has been interpreted in history as an independent, sentient being. It presents the view that this is no longer tenable, and that the Christian God should be recognised as an image which has been created and sustained by the human mind to meet human needs.

Ludvic Kennedy examines the origin of gods, questions the reliability of the bible, and records the growth of atheism and changes in Church behaviour in Europe. Much may be familiar to the life-long Humanist, but the potential of this book is to appeal to a wider audience. Being written by a well known personality must also enable it to be more widely read. The real appeal of the book, however, is in sharing the personal impact of religion on the author's life, as he grew up in a British Christian background and came to question its philosophy. *RM*

(All in the Mind by Ludvic Kennedy see Bibliography on page 92.)

43

Humanism in Australia

Australian Humanist societies are affiliated to the national body, the Council of Australian Humanist Societies (CAHS), which is a member of IHEU. CAHS holds an annual convention, publishes the quarterly journal, *Australian Humanist*, and presents the Australian Humanist of the Year award.

Humanists in Australia campaign for greater equality, and fair treatment to disadvantaged groups such as Aborigines, ethnic minorities, the disabled and unemployed. They seek secular schooling for all children in the interests of greater acceptance and tolerance. Locally, Humanist societies discuss and exchange ideas; produce regular journals with members' views, opinions and reports; hold a variety of social events as well as lobbying state and federal governments on important issues of the day.

Universal problems of over-population, species survival, third world exploitation and environmental degradation are addressed by Humanists who help in trying to find a solution to these world-wide problems.*(details: http://home.vicnet.net.au/~humanist/cahs)*

* * * * *

Humanism in New Zealand

The Humanist Society of New Zealand was founded in 1967 as a development from the Rationalist Association. It also stemmed from the Auckland University Humanist Society. New branches formed, and existing groups became affiliated to the HSNZ, which became an associate member of IHEU. A Humanist library was set up and a Humanist bookshop established.

Locally, Humanist branches meet regularly to discuss and exchange ideas with people of like minds, to hear speakers on Humanist philosophy, other belief systems and social issues. Branches organise projects such as the settlement of refugees, hospital visiting, Access Radio programmes and social gatherings. Nationally, the Society produces the quarterly magazine, launched in 1970, *New Zealand Humanist*, and issues regular newsletters to 'lone' and branch members. Seminars are organised and representation is made to government and public bodies.

(See Bibliography page 92 for details of HSNZ's 25th anniversary book.)

What's in a name?

Days, months, festivals and ceremonies have been named, renamed and adapted. The days were named after the seven (known) planets, and later some were changed to their appropriate planet-gods or goddesses. Surviving roots can be seen with Solis Dies, Sunday, and in Moon's day and Saturn's day. The months were altered and renamed after gods, goddesses, the Caesars or just called fifth to the tenth, the original month of March having started the new year.

Traditional festivities, celebrations and superstitions, seldom disappeared altogether, as they assumed new forms and adapted to new conditions. In pre-history, celebrations were held for the simple desire to welcome back the reviving sun, because there was no way of knowing when or if it would return. Saturnalia, the Roman Kalends and special feast days developed, houses were decorated, games were played and presents were given.

Over time, with the developing calendar, these festivities and traditions began to merge, so that when the Christian church came into being the pagan ceremonies were incorporated into Christian festivals to make transition easier for converted heathens. Later, this midwinter festival became a celebration for the birthday of Jesus, but all the decorations with their pagan, heathen origins had to be taken down by the twelfth night for the Church's celebration of Epiphany. A combination of many festivals and traditions during midwinter eventually emerged with the name *Christmas*.

From early pagan roots came belief in a goddess of nature, that created new life at the time of the vernal equinox. Celebrations expressed thanks for germinating seeds, new birth and hope of flourishing crops to come. Many variations of this goddess existed. Ostara was the northern form of Astarte, Lady of Byblos, the great goddess of the Middle East who was identified with Egypt's Hathor, Mycenae's Demeter and Cyprus's Aphrodite.

Later, in Saxon times, the goddess was known as Eostre, and from this root comes the English word *Easter.* Because of sharing pagan roots in a dating system based on the old lunar calendar, Easter is a movable feast day. The date is fixed as the first Sunday after the first full moon of the Spring Equinox. This was once considered to be the pregnant phase of Eostre, when she passed into the fertile season.

Halloween, or All Hallows' Eve, marks the evening before All Hallows' Day, the ancient festival of the dead. For the Celts it was the eve of their New Year, called Samhain, when celebrations marked the ending of the old and beginning of the new. They believed that ghosts of the dead were able to mingle with the living, before their souls travelled into another world.

The Romans held a festival in honour of the goddess of fruits and gardens at this time, and a festival of fire was also celebrated. As Christianity developed, earlier celebrations were combined into Christian celebrations, so that by retaining many pagan practices pagans could be absorbed into the new religion. Hallowmas or All Hallows Day became All Saints Day, which precedes All Soul's Day, and Halloween emerged from a mixture of these roots with the superstitions of ghosts, witches and spirits appearing.

Today we carry on the convenience of using the traditional names of days, months and celebrations, without necessarily thinking of their multi-purpose origins. It would be unthinkable to change the days or months, but sometimes earlier names for the midwinter festival are used, and new ones devised like Winterval.

* * * * *

Evolution

The implications of evolution have affected the way we view life and our beliefs, because of the growth of awareness since the early 19th century. Geology and biology reveal overwhelming supportive evidence through fossil records indicating millions of years of development of life. Evolution shatters the credibility of many religious doctrines and superstitions, but it still presents dilemmas for mankind to face.

How do we reconcile evolution's concept of ruthless survival of the fittest with our instinct for compassion and co-operation? How much free will do we really have to control our destiny, in the face of natural forces? Might our current wasteful use of resources, short term interests and specialised lifestyle indicate that we may posses the seeds of our own destruction?

With evolution, many life forms thrived, lost their adaptability and became extinct as other forms overtook them. But humans are conscious of evolution, so it is our responsibility to try to improve the quality and sustainability of life on earth. *RM*

46

Background to the —

South Place Ethical Society

In the late 17th century, a new ethos of religious thought began to supersede the Calvinism which dominated English non-comformity. Intolerance, bloodshed and violence in religious controversy had left a feeling of revulsion.

A growing belief developed amongst dissenters that man must be guided solely by his reason and conscience, and not by received doctrine of the Church which offended common and moral sense. From these roots emerged the Universalists. From the Universalists emerged the Unitarians and ultimately South Place, where gradually a centre of advanced and progressive thought was established.

A start was made by a few dissenters in 1793, led by Elhanan Winchester, an American Universalist. But more radical changes came with Winchester's successor, William Vidler, who discarded most of his non-conformist Baptist beliefs for Unitarianism. Thus the doctrines of original sin, the atonement, justification by faith, predestination, the trinity and everlasting punishment were gradually rejected, even though it was a punishable offence to deny the 'truth' of the three-in-one trinity. This law was only repealed in 1813.

William Johnson Fox, a non-conformist who became a Unitarian, was next to lead the growing band of dissenters from 1817. He was concerned with social reform, in particular education for all and repeal of the Corn Laws. By 1823 the Society moved to its new purpose-built building, South Place, in Finsbury, where it stayed for over a hundred years. William Fox was elected to parliament in 1847, although he continued his work at South Place.

It wasn't until Moncure Conway arrived in England in 1863 that the quasi-religious ethos of South Place began to change. Conway, a Virginian who had fought against slavery, had a Methodist/Unitarian background, but his studies in comparative religion and anthropology had altered his way of thinking, so that he found he could no longer use his old American sermons. Prior to his appointment, the Sunday procedure at South Place had followed a non-conformist pattern, but Conway quickly introduced an alternative to the regular bible reading and had meditative readings instead of prayers.

It has been said of Conway that, 'His Humanism was positive and wholly rational. The study of anthropology and folklore had more than anything else to do with the shaping of his maturer thought.' Of his own sermons, he said that they ceased to be theological and had become anthropological. Lectures during the week were now given by many notable speakers and South Place gained a reputation as a pioneer centre of adult education.

Conway retired after twenty-two years and was succeeded for four years by Stanton Coit, also an American, who changed the name of South Place from 'religious' to 'ethical'. He also introduced Sunday chamber music concerts, at a time when entertainment on Sundays wasn't considered correct. But they became immensely popular and well respected in the musical world as each year, from October to April, the concerts helped to bring an understanding and enjoyment of music to many who would otherwise not hear it. When Stanton Coit resigned, he went on to be leader of the West London Ethical Society, and Moncure Conway returned to South Place for a further five years.

During this time the forerunner of the Society's present magazine was started and continued through two changes of name before becoming the *Ethical Record* in 1965. When Conway finally retired, the committee appointed four regular lecturers. And soon supplementary lectures on Sundays and weekdays were given by an increasing number of eminent speakers including Ramsey McDonald, Bernard Shaw and Alfred Russel Wallace.

Conway Memorial Lectures were endowed to enable an annual lecture to be given each autumn. The growing list of speakers later included James Hemming, Marghanita Laski, Edmund Leach, Jonathan Miller, Laurens van der Post and many more notable speakers whose talks were printed in booklet form.

South Place in Finsbury was sold, and the Society moved to Red Lion Square in 1929. The move acted as a stimulus as membership increased and new discussion and study groups were formed. Despite the depression and imminence of the Second World War, a high standard of lectures, discussions and concerts was maintained in the new hall that housed 500. Today, the Society continues to give lectures and concerts, publishes the *Ethical Record*, and provides a forum for social controversies in helping to promote the open society.

(The Story of South Place see Bibliography page 92 and Contacts page 93.)

Dates to conjure with

There were only 304 days in the Roman year before 700BCE, when it was amended to 355 (approximating to the lunar year). In 46/45BCE, with philosophers, mathematicians and astronomers, Julius Caesar changed it again, in line with the even earlier Egyptian calendar of Ptolemy III — with 365 and a quarter days, the fraction being taken up by a leap year every fourth year.

To bring the calendar back in line with the Vernal Equinox, which had traditionally fallen on 25th March, Caesar ordered an extra eighty days to be added to 46BCE. Not surprisingly, this became known as the 'Year of Confusion'. At the same time, he moved the first day of the year from March to January, nearer the Winter Solstice, with the new calendar starting on January the 1st 45BCE.

At this time February had twenty-nine days for three years, then thirty in a leap year. The following year, after Caesar's death, leap years came every three years, but the mistake wasn't seen until 8BCE when it was adjusted so that there were no leap years until 8CE. To honour Caesar, the month called Quintilius (original fifth month) was changed to Julius (July), and further changes came when Sextilius (sixth month) was renamed Augustus to honour the new Caesar. But because Julius had thirty-one days, Augustus was also given thirty-one, by taking one day from February. The number of days in September to December were also rearranged, to avoid three months of thirty-one days following each other. All this upset the neatly alternating thirty and thirty-one days.

In 525 Pope John 1 sent for an abbot, Dionysus Exiguus, to work out the date for the following Easter. As head of the Roman Christians, Pope John did not like having to rely on the 'other' Christian church, the Coptics in Alexandria, because they created a mystery about how the date was worked out, saying they were the only ones who understood it.

Dionysus, known for his work on calendars and Catholic rules or canons, was also a mathematician and not only worked out the date of the next Easter, but six years later had established the next ninety-six. He based his chart on a nineteen-year cycle of moon phases, arbitrarily set by using the old Roman system of Kalends,

Ides and Nones. Dates were calculated from the beginning of the reign of Diocletian, but as Diocletian had persecuted the Christians, Dionysus changed the dating system to the estimated birth of Jesus. He calculated this to be 531 years earlier. So the following year, 247 *Anno Diocletiani* became *Anno Domini Jesu Christi* 532. How this date was determined has caused controversy ever since. A further anomaly was created because there is no year zero as the concept of zero was unknown.

By the mid 13th century the calendar year was calculated to be eleven minutes longer than the solar year. If left unchecked the actual months would 'slip back'. Roger Bacon, a friar, pointed out that Easter was being celebrated on the wrong day because it was calculated by the spring equinox — and equinoxes, like solstices, were placed on fixed days. After many endeavours to reform the calendar, Bacon was charged with 'espousing suspected novelties', and people were forbidden to study his 'dangerous teaching'.

In 1582 the calendar was reformed once more, this time by Pope Gregory XIII, who removed ten days to realign it with the solar year. Most Catholic countries accepted the Gregorian calendar within two years, but Protestants opposed the change, arguing that it was 'against nature' and 'real Christians' would be worshipping on the incorrect holy days. Many people thought the Pope had *stolen* the ten days.

Others said birds were confused about when they should sing or fly away. Catholics countered by saying a nut tree had responded to the Papal reform by blossoming ten days early. A main inconvenience was that someone travelling from a Catholic country on January 1st could arrive in a Protestant one on December 21st the previous year!

It was not until 1752 that Britain (and American colonies) accepted the 'new' calendar by eliminating eleven days from the Julian calendar so that September 14th followed September 2nd. Once again, people thought days had been 'stolen', and some demonstrated with placards saying, 'Give us back our eleven days'. This time, a Glastonbury thorn was said to have 'contemptuously ignored the new style and burst into bloom on the 5th January', instead of on Christmas Day as before.

Valued lives
Marie Curie — *1867-1934*

Marie Curie was born in Warsaw as Marya Sklodowska. As a child she was called Manya by her parents, older brother and three sisters. Her father was professor of physics and under-inspector of the High School for Boys, where the family lived. Their mother, also a professor, had worked at the private school where she had been educated and became its director until the family moved to the High School.

Manya had learnt to read with the help of her sister, who was also learning. But education for girls of four was discouraged to prevent *precocity*. Despite this, Manya's astonishing memory gave her an absorbing interest in everything around her, particularly the glass fronted case of 'physics apparatus' in her father's study.

Repression through Russian rule, with smouldering resentment which had twice erupted, meant lessons were conducted in Russian. But clandestine classes took place in the private boarding school which the Sklodowska sisters attended, and where Manya was by two years the youngest in her class. When a double bell sounded all Polish books hastily 'disappeared', so by the time the outside inspector arrived he found a 'needlework class' in progress. And Manya, with her good memory and fluent Russian, was picked to answer the inspector's questions on Russian history.

But lies, deceit, repression and the unhappiness caused by her mother's terminal tuberculosis, her father's unfair demotion and the death of one of her sisters through typhoid, caused great grief and suffering to little Manya. The cruelty, grief and unfairness of life turned her away from the god she had once believed in. But her early background, mixed with repression and sorrow, gave her the strength of character to fight any obstacle that beset her.

Through contacts with 'Positivists', she extended her education through the secret Floating University, and in turn helped those who lacked Polish education. The only chance of entering a university was in Paris, but money wouldn't allow it. So Manya devised a plan whereby her older sister could take a medical training in Paris, while Manya became a governess to help pay for her. Then, when trained, her sister could help Manya go to the Sorbonne.

During the three years Manya worked as a governess, she also taught local children basic literacy and did her own private studies. Three more years went by as she struggled to raise money. Finally, in 1891, she took a three-day train journey to continue her study and achieve her aspirations.

In Paris, Manya emerged as Maria, and after two poverty-stricken years she received a scholarship to complete her studies. In 1894 she met her husband-to-be, Pierre Curie, the eminent French physicist, and they were married the following year. Pierre was a freethinker and Marie had lost her religious belief, so their marriage was unconventional, with no religious service.

By 1897 Marie had two degrees, a fellowship, a monograph on magnetism — and their first child. She went on to take her doctorate in a fundamental study of uranium rays with the resultant discovery of radium. In 1903, Henri Becquerel and Pierre and Marie Curie shared the Nobel Prize for their work on radioactivity. The full story of Maria Currie is one of determination against all odds. But her first principle was 'never let oneself be beaten down by persons or events'.

* * * * *

Enjoy . . .

Driving back from Sussex, at 6 o'clock one August Bank Holiday morning, I was struck again by the beauty of our country. At that time there was little traffic as people had already made their journeys westwards for the last week of the summer holidays. There are few congestions now where tired traffic once crawled through clogged towns and villages. Bypasses and new road layouts not only make driving easier, but open up the countryside for all to see.

It spread out around me, hills fresh and sparkling in the early morning sun; fields that really are like patchwork; here and there a group of mottled rooftops half-hidden by clusters of trees; and far beyond, a glint of grey-blue sea stretching to the horizon. The pictures constantly changed as I travelled on through peaceful Dorset to the more rugged landscape of Devon.

Romantic view? Well, maybe. But life is *now*, and we can't constantly be thinking of the horrors of civil war and the tragedies of earthquakes and hurricanes. These are real enough and are continually voiced. So I enjoyed the beauty of the moment and revelled in the natural world of which we are so lucky to be a part.

Humanist ceremonies

In Britain, today, about half of all weddings are still conducted in a place of worship. Of these, we do not know how many are the weddings of couples who hold no religious beliefs, but we can hazard a guess that the number is high. However, to take part in an overtly religious ceremony is likely to be an uncomfortable, if not distasteful, experience for those who have no belief in a god.

The Humanist concept of a wedding ceremony is distinctive. It illustrates important values and beliefs while giving expression to two people's personalities. Moreover, there is a flexibility and openness of approach that is quite unusual. Remarriage after divorce, the marriage of couples where children from earlier relationships are included, weddings where the bride does not wish to be 'given away' by her father or to take her new husband's name — all kinds of different situations can be accommodated.

The current legal position is extremely unsatisfactory in that it discriminates against those whose beliefs do not include worship of a god. Humanism has no worship, fixed rituals or dogmatic rules other than the desire that each of us should make the most of life, and try to benefit other people while we're doing so.

Baby naming ceremonies are chosen by many different families: two married parents, two unmarried parents, single parents, adoptive parents, step parents, parents who are of different religions or cultures, and lesbian or gay couples with children. Occasionally a Humanist wedding is held at the same time.

Each naming ceremony is unique because no set pattern or script must be followed, so parents are able to choose every aspect of the ceremony. This is what so many parents value. Since the ceremony is non-religious the phrase 'godparents' is not appropriate. But there is still a useful role that can be played by one or two friends or relatives. What to call them is more difficult. Some people like words such as 'sponsor', 'mentor', 'supporter' or 'special friend'.

The role of a supporting adult is to take a special interest in the child's development and support the parents throughout the long years until the child is adult, and to be there as a listening ear and welcome source of advice for the child outside the immediate family. Humanist baby namings, weddings and funerals are inclusive. The ceremonies are based on what we all have in common — our humanity and human values — and this transcends any religious beliefs that some of the people present may have.

There are more and more people for whom religion is less important or who have made a clear decision to live their lives without it. For them, a religious funeral service may seem insincere and bring little consolation. It may not feel the right way to say their final farewell to someone who did not accept the religious view of life and death. In this case it is likely to have more warmth and meaning if the ceremony is of the kind favoured by the British Humanist Association's officiants.

Humanist officiants come from a variety of backgrounds. What they share is an ability to empathise with the experience of bereavement. They are men and women, trained by BHA, who are familiar with the procedures of cremation and burial. They need to be good interviewers and attentive listeners; sensitive to the family's wishes, yet ready to give clear guidance as needed; able to prepare and take charge of a solemn public occasion.

We find that religious people often comment on how inspiring Humanist ceremonies are, and how closely they could relate to all that took place. In other words, while being definitely non-religious, Humanism aims to speak for everyone. *JWW*
(Compiled from New Arrivals, Sharing the Future and Funerals Without God by Jane Wynne Willson for details see Bibliography on page 92.)

* * * * *

Potted profile — 4

In 1955, when Margaret Knight (1903-1983) gave three BBC radio talks on non-religious morality and education, there was an outcry from some sections of the public and press. But it opened the once firmly closed door to a wider reception. The talks were included in her collection of essays, *Morals Without Religion*. Margaret Knight worked with her husband, Professor Rex Knight, in the psychology department of Aberdeen University. Together they wrote *A Modern Introduction to Psychology*. She was an active speaker and writer for the Humanist movement, and wrote *Religion and Your Child*: a symposium of problems of Humanist parents. In 1961 Margaret Knight edited the first edition of *A Humanist Anthology*. This was revised and reissued in 1995.
(Details of Margaret Knight's books are in the Bibliography on page 92.)

Values

"What I cannot understand about you Humanists," a clergyman said to me one day, "is how you can go through life refusing to believe in the existence of good and evil."

"We believe, of course, in better or worse," I replied, "but I suppose you mean God and the devil: absolute good and absolute evil."

"You cannot have comparatives without absolutes," was his parting shot.

In nature, however, everything is relative; there are no absolutes. Ten miles is longer than nine miles, but is there an absolute longest?

The idea of absolute perfection, against which everything else must be measured, is part of the whole religious concept of some other reality behind the reality we experience — a concept which Christianity took over from Platonic philosophy.

According to this idea, all the goodness, beauty and truth in this world are reflections of Goodness, Beauty and Truth in another ideal world, which Christians call heaven from whence, they say, all human values derive. Humanism, on the other hand, recognises no values for human beings to live by that are not derived from human experience.

But we are left with the philosophical problem of how we judge that one thing is better than another. Is it no more than a matter of taste? Bertrand Russell, after a lifetime immersed in philosophy, was still, in his late eighties, looking for a solution to the problem. "I find myself incapable of believing," he said. "that all that is wrong with wanton cruelty is that I don't like it."

To most of us, it is self-evident that it is better for sentient beings to experience pleasure and happiness than pain and misery, and that kindness is therefore good and cruelty bad.

Biologically, the desire to avoid pain and misery evolved as important survival factors, and we are the product of our evolutionary past. The animal desire, inbred in us to avoid pain and misery, reaches a high point in human sensibility, and it is this sensibility that gives us our moral and aesthetic values. *BS*
(From chapter four, Values — good and bad, taken from Humanism by Barbara Smoker. For details see Bibliography on page 92.)

Consumer populism

During a lifetime in journalism, John Humphrys has observed the changes overtaking Britain. He has used this experience to set them in context by challenging social and moral values, and questioning the direction society is taking. He feels that everything is geared to marketing and getting the public to buy. Subtly done, we see ourselves as 'victims', and the only way to alleviate our loss of status is to buy more to achieve temporary satisfaction.

John Humphrys' book, *Devil's Advocate*, is a realistic appraisal of modern life, showing how we have turned from being individual citizens to a consumer orientated society. The book is divided into three parts. The first sets out, in his lucid, readable way, the climate of opinion that prevails today and the way in which 'the notion of responsibility has changed over the past forty years'. The second part shows how 'the two great engines of consumer populism - commercialism and the media - have helped make us the people we are'. The third section addresses the question, 'What's to be done about it?'

We are living, John Humphrys says, in a 'blame society' where, when things go wrong it is usually seen as someone else's fault, because the whole point of consumer populism is that it fights against the idea of individual responsibility:

> Consumer populism cheapens, coarsens, makes false promises and offers phoney solutions and I think we should make a fuss about it.

His approach is humanistic in wanting us all to think about how attitudes have changed, and to understand the cramping effect commercialism already has on society. But he says, 'If any small boy dares shout that the emperor has no clothes he is condemned as a Philistine.' However, daring to be different and daring not to accept without question are attributes that are capable of breaking the strong hold that consumer populism increasingly exerts.

Pointing out where and why the world is going wrong doesn't make this a negative book. Far from it, because within its pages are many optimistic signs that we are beginning to realise what is happening and starting to do something about it.

(Devil's Advocate by John Humphrys see Bibliography on page 92.)

Background to the —

Rationalist Press Association

The Rationalist Press Association (RPA) stems from freethought and social, political and religious reform. In 1817, Richard Carlile (1790-1843) took over a radical publishing company and concentrated on religious criticism rather than political. Meanwhile, the mass movement of social and political reform was stirring. Robert Owen (1771-1858) created a model community, contending that character was formed by social environment. The community had a village store (forerunner of the Co-op), a school, evening classes, the world's first day nursery and playground and the 'Institution for the Formation of Character'.

When the Owenites' movement declined during the 1830s, many of its members continued campaigning against Christianity. They emerged from *rational* religion to no religion. George Jacob Holyoake (1817-1906) lectured on the social reforms of Robert Owen and edited the *Oracle of Reason*. He was imprisoned for blasphemy, as had Richard Carlile and his family and colleagues many years earlier. Other editors of freethought periodicals were also imprisoned, but Holyoake was the last person to be sentenced in England on a charge of atheism (1842). However, he determined not only to produce literature, but to provide a proper identity for the freethought movement. He adopted the word 'secularism' in 1851, and began forming secular societies.

During this time, Richard Carlile's publishing firm had passed to James Watson and in 1854 it was sold to Austin Holyoake. Charles Bradlaugh succeeded G.J. Holyoake in the secularist movement that founded the National Secular Society (see pages 73-4). Meanwhile, G.J. Holyoake continued to campaign and write for freethought and electoral reform. Over this period, John and Charles Watts, sons of a Methodist minister, had taken leading parts in the freethought movement. Charles Watts took over the printing firm from Austin Holyoake in 1874 and produced the *Secular Review*.

In 1877, due to a split in the secularist movement over Malthusianism, Charles Watts and George J Holyoake came together with the more moderate secularists. In 1878 they formed the British Secular Union (BSU), with the Marquis of Queensbury as the first president. Sadly, the new venture declined when Charles Watts settled in Canada in 1884. The printing business passed to his son Charles Albert (1858-1946), who had been apprenticed to Austin Holyoake at the age of twelve. He was also a committee member of the BSU and sub-editor of the *Secular Review*.

An agnostic movement, inspired by Herbert Spencer and Thomas Huxley (who coined the word agnosticism) filled a temporary gap producing many non-religious and quasi-religious publications. Charles Albert Watts was also active in this movement. He produced the *Agnostic Almanack* in 1883, which became the *Agnostic Annual* and later the *Rationalist Annual*. He also produced a new monthly paper called the *Agnostic* which, with two changes of name, continued and became an established feature of the freethought movement until Charles Albert's death.

Another facet of RPA's background was through the Ethical movement (see page 16). Charles Albert Watts was sympathetic to their ideas and published the *Ethical World* for the Union of Ethical Societies. But his greatest interest was in forming the Propagandist Press Committee to support literature on 'Freethought and Advanced Religious Reform'. In 1893 this became the Rationalist Press Committee to support 'the production and circulation of Rationalist publications'.

In May 1899, the Rationalist Press Committee became the Rationalist Press Association (RPA) as a limited company, by following the example of NSS. Both organisations were thus set on firm foundations for the future. G.J. Holyoake became the first president of RPA, and after returning from Canada Charles Watts became a supporter, together with many notable freethinkers and secularists. RPA shared the premises of Watts and Co. which, although a separate entity, collaborated in printing and publishing literature for RPA.

The original intention, to provide a financial basis for freethought publishing, was thus fulfilled. Besides publishing, RPA developed a library and held public lectures and meetings for members, who had increased from the original 100 to 5,000 by 1947. In 1962 RPA became an educational charity (until 1971), which helped pave the way to founding BHA jointly with the Ethical Union. Today, although membership has declined, RPA continues to publish books of Humanist interest and to produce a more prestigious quarterly magazine, *New Humanist*.

(See Contacts on page 93.)

Touch wood . . .

Superstitions have been described as a form of personal magic used for coming to terms with the unknown. With the once great dependence on agriculture, many superstitions have a rustic bias. Primitive people could not explain why the rain came that helped their crops to grow or why the sun returned to them each year, so they devised ways of trying to avert the many risks and dangers that threatened their survival.

Rituals grew up around their felt need to invoke unseen powers into providing food and protection, and gradually these became woven into inherited traditions. The early history of mankind was shaped and dominated by superstitious beliefs which continued to be passed on and adapted. At the same time, its language became embedded in the culture of different societies.

From the unseen powers of protection, gradually emerged gods. These 'protectors' were given divine and magical powers capable of destroying life or ensuring its continuance. In time, the good and bad influences were separated, giving the 'bad' a distinct identity as Satan or the Devil. The cross developed as a good luck symbol, but in Puritan times, when crosses were forbidden, people crossed their fingers out of sight instead. Crossing fingers then became a talisman for warding off danger or encouraging good luck. Today, children sometimes cross their fingers when telling lies — and crossing fingers is perpetuated by the National Lottery symbol. Touching wood represents touching the wooden cross to invoke good luck or ward off bad.

Walking under a ladder was once thought to break the triangle of God, the spirit and man. Passing someone on the stairs is symbolic of walking up the ladder in Jacob's dream and stepping on the same stair as one of the angels that had been 'ascending and descending', thus incurring the wrath of God. However, people passing on the stairs can be protected by crossing their fingers! Friday the 13th is said to be unlucky because it represents the Last Supper. "Bless you", is said when someone sneezes because sneezing heralded the plague.

Superstitions abound, but many original meanings, with their roots embedded in ancient cultures, are in danger of being lost.

Biker's funeral

Before breakfast, one Thursday in summer, a funeral director phoned to ask if I would take the funeral of a local biker killed in a road accident two weeks earlier. His friends had planned to take the ceremony but at the last minute decided they needed help. I was that help — and the funeral was to be in two days time.

I agreed to meet the *Devon Chapter of Satan's Slaves* at 9pm at their club, a local pub, which I was told was the safest pub in town because it was run by the roughest people. I was met by bearded bikers, tattooed and wearing their leathers. They were *not* rough and I saw nothing but caring, gentleness and kindness both to each other and to me. And like the biker who had died, they were non-smokers and teetotal.

Much of the funeral planning was already organised. They had a printed order of ceremony with chosen music and speakers, and they had organised their own sound system at the crematorium. A double slot at the crematorium was booked, and everyone knew what they wanted and how it was to run. I was to do the 'joining bits' to make it run smoothly and professionally.

From the pub to the crematorium a cavalcade of 250 bikers, following a lorry banked with flowers, was escorted by the police. Other bikers, some from New Zealand, made their way to the chapel along roads lined with waiting people. The cavalcade arrived about forty minutes early because nobody had considered that with a police escort their journey would be very rapid, with all the traffic lights geared to their progress and the flow of other traffic halted.

The chapel was full to bursting with another 500 people outside. Music chosen for the ceremony included a piece by the Hollies, then John Lennon's *Imagine*, and the closing track was a modern version of a Samuel Barber piece. Six speakers, all moved by the occasion, struggled with their own grief. But it was a good ceremony, with caring people saying their farewells to their leader and friend.

The fellowship demonstrated between people from all over the world was to be envied. Once again I learned that what you think you see is not necessarily what you get, because for me I found new friends. *CM*

Humanism in Europe

Humanist and freethinking organisations are spread widely across Europe, many of which are members of IHEU representing groups from Austria, Belgium, Finland, France, Germany, Greece, Hungary, Ireland, Italy, Luxembourg, the Netherlands, Norway, Poland, Slovakia, Sweden and Switzerland. Activities vary, but most associations have local groups and educational programmes.

In 1945, the initiatives of Drs. J.P. van Praag and J in't Veld in the Netherlands led to the formation of Humanitas, an organisation concerned with practical social work. The following year Humanistisch Verbond (the Dutch Humanist Ethical Society) and Humanistisch Verbond Belgie were established. Today, the two main Dutch organisations have around 15,000 members each, with some overlapping. Humanitas is involved with childcare, homes for the elderly and working with the disabled, lonely and homeless. Because state law allows free pastoral care, 100 hospitals and nursing homes are able to employ pastoral care workers and eighty are employed by the army and in prisons.

German Humanists are regionally focussed, with representatives constituting the national association. In Berlin parents of primary school children choose for their child either religious studies or Lebenskunde (or neither activity). Lebenskunde is pupil centred to answer questions on morality based on reason and human experience. The Berlin Humanist Association employs and trains 150 teachers for the allocated two hours a week curriculum time. About 24,000 pupils follow this programme of study and even though many drop out when they are about twelve, by fourteen those who continue take part in Jugendfeier, the civic youth celebrations to celebrate 'coming of age' which has become an important festivity for freethinkers.

Humanisterna (formerly Human-Etiska Forbundet) the Swedish Humanist Association, created in 1979, arranges similar coming of age celebrations for young people each summer at Humanist confirmation camps. As a result of this interest the quarterly journal *Humanisten* now publishes special youth pages. Jonge Humanisten is a meeting place for young people in the Netherlands with activities, discussions and a regular newsletter. Humanist literature, magazines and newsletters are produced in

63

most countries, and some organisations publish books.

The Prometheus Society of Slovakia was formed in 1990 with aims 'to spread and defend freethinking and support Humanism and the principle of tolerance'. The following year, the group became a member of IHEU, together with the Hungarian Humanist Association and Poland's Secular Culture Society. Also in 1991 the Polish Humanist Association was formed. A Polish edition of *Espace de Liberté*, produced by the Belgian Centre d'Action Laique, was distributed to Polish universities and, through the initiative of Dutch Humanists and West Europe's educational fund, Polish teachers were trained to teach Humanist ethical education as an alternative to Catholic lessons in school.

(European details are on the IHEU website see Contacts on page 93.)

* * * * *

Future of humanity

'Designer babies', 'genetically enhanced humans', 'bright, shiny genetic future' are phrases that have been banded around since the announcement that the human genome had been decoded. There is also talk of banishing hereditary illnesses, and that parents will be able to choose the attributes of their children. Underlying this is the word eugenics, with its uncomfortable memories of promoting superior beings and eliminating inferior ones. Eugenics has already caused missing generations of girls because some cultures thought boys more useful or superior.

One issue raised is whether it would be desirable for the long-term health of the species to eliminate so called undesirable human genes, since some weaknesses in one area cause a stronger, compensatory effect in another. Nobel Prize winners, many from humble backgrounds, and geniuses in varied fields, don't necessarily produce similar geniuses, so eliminating certain genes without knowing future needs would restrict potential variation.

An article in *Nature Genetics* argued that, 'It makes no sense to drive our species into a man-made bottle-neck of genetic uniformity.' And the way we judge the value of genes is 'biased, myopic and only relevant to the present'. It is not known what kind of gene variant will be needed in the future, since today's needs are different from those of stone-age man. The debate has a long and interesting future. Hopefully the human species will too, without becoming the outcasts of John Wyndham's *Chrysalids*.

Strange encounter

I was alone, busily working on my allotment, when I saw a mother and young boy coming towards me over the rutted path.

"Sorry to disturb you," said the mother, as they neared. "We won't keep you long."

The boy, clutching a clip board, came forward. Perhaps he's doing a project on allotments I thought, noting his tie and smart shirt. But as he started to speak I recognised a familiar pattern.

"Where are you from?" I casually interrupted.

"Teignmouth," he said.

"No, I mean which organisation?"

"The Jehovah's Witness."

"Ah, yes," I said, smiling, "I thought so."

Nervously, he carried on with his rehearsed talk, repeatedly quoting from a magazine. But all the while my mind was saying, this isn't right. Why should a young boy be out here in the middle of overgrown allotments trying to convert a woman five times his age? What knowledge has he? What experience of life? I let him continue, then turned to his mother.

"Is it fair that he should be doing this?" I said, quietly. "How old is he?"

"Ask him," she said, "he's an intelligent chap."

"Twelve," said the boy.

"He has a lot of learning to do," I said to the mother.

I could have tied him in theological and philosophical knots. But it wasn't fair. It wasn't right. It wasn't *kind*. He was already being unduly exploited, so to take further advantage of his tender years would be cruel. I simply turned to him and said, "That may be your viewpoint, but I'm a Humanist and mine is different."

"Thank you for sparing your time," said the mother, hastily.

"Thank you for sparing your time," echoed the boy.

We all said goodbye and I watched them walking back over the rough path to the country lane where there were no houses. I felt desperately sorry for the boy, coming to a distant allotment to practise verbal communication. I thought it must have been the mother's idea, for surely no organisation would use a twelve year old to evangelise for them? My hope was that having started so young the boy would soon begin to think for himself.

65

Sporting chance

All sports are keen to defend their image and come down heavily on drug-taking, for example, and corruption of all kinds. Nevertheless, we have almost become accustomed to expect there to be 'goings on' in most sports, except that most English of them all, cricket. The expression, 'It's not cricket.' epitomises the game as an icon of high standards of personal conduct and fair play. Regrettably, and amid much media hype, it has been brought into disrepute by accusations of match-fixing and bribery.

A sense of fairness seems to be one of those attributes which is peculiar to the human race. The runt of the litter can expect scant consideration from its siblings or even its mother; the newly hatched cuckoo loses no time in tipping the remaining eggs unceremoniously out of the nest; 'Red in tooth and claw' as Tennyson put it, is what we expect from the rest of nature. But from our own species we have higher expectations, and it is a defining moment in every child's life when s/he first wails, 'But it's not fair.' Okay, so fairness, like beauty is often in the eyes of the beholder, and is frequently a self-serving plea, but it is also the fundamental motive for the existence of almost every well-meaning charity you can think of.

It is not a fair world, of course, and probably never will be. Unfairness in terms of inequality of opportunity, of access to healthcare, education, adequate nourishment even, is a fact of life for many of Earth's six billion human inhabitants. But many of us reach out from the security of our assured well-being to try to redress the balance for one segment or other of the world's disadvantaged, and we do so in the name of fairness.

To return to cricket, that incomprehensible game where those who are out go in, those who are next in go out, and where 'drawn game' doesn't even mean the scores are equal. Cricket is a microcosm of the struggle between fairness and survival: the rules are complex, team strategies are of the essence, and there are — or always have been — expectations of admirable behaviour. For it to be sullied by 'unsporting activities' is a loss not only to cricket, but to idealism in general. We all need encouragement to 'play up, play up and play the game', as Sir Henry Newbolt put it. Without such icons as cricket, cynicism too easily sets in. *RL*

Born or made

The complexity of bee hives, flocks of birds, the rich culture of meadows and even evolving viruses are natural examples of interconnecting ecosystems. Human life and our interdependence on each other can be equated in a similar way, because we are beginning to act as a 'flock'. Not because we are regimented into doing so, but because each activity affects the wider community and is itself interdependent on many unseen influences.

We are also constantly striving towards a more mechanised world, and the more we use machines and technology for our own benefit, the more interdependent we become, losing control to the 'superorganism' of mechanical-humanity. Machines are acting as 'people', but people with far quicker reaction times and stamina. With self-repair and self-regulation could they also evolve self-consciousness? This is the suggestion posed by Kevin Kelly in his fascinating and very readable book, *Out of Control*.

But in the past, evolution — and ultimate extinction — occurred without conscious interference. By creating machines with 'intelligence' could we be creating our own demise? We can influence, but we cannot control the interconnections of the biosphere which has no controller, since its total make-up is interdependent. If we are already 'out of control' because of this interdependency, will our technology create machines that decide to dominate, thus having no need for the natural world of which we are a part? Kevin Kelly thinks not, because 'life is the ultimate technology' and machine technology is a 'temporary surrogate'.

In the boundary between 'born and made', humans are striving to close the gap. It is not a question of machines taking over, but humans creating machines and systems that copy and adapt natural processes which have evolved through the complexities of nature. (But is there any reason why humans are necessarily the ultimate stage of evolution?)

Nature is super efficient in its economy and use of its natural resources. Humans are wasteful. To create a similarly super efficient economy of resources, humans need to refine machines and technology to be as efficient as their natural counterpart. It could be done. The book makes fascinating reading.

(Out of Control by Kevin Kelly see Bibliography on page 92.)

I'm right, you're wrong

How we talk with each other, and *why* we talk, lies at the heart of what we feel about ourselves as well as others. We present ourselves to the world in many ways. But all these perceptions can totally change the moment we open our mouths and speak.

As we grow up, we internalise and employ many different strategies when we talk with others. Most of us do not spend time reflecting on how we talk. We tend just to talk. Although it seems that our capacity to use language is, in many ways, a kind of instinct which is unique to human beings, language is itself symbolic, in that it represents experience.

Babies' earliest speech utterances are essentially expressive rather than intentionally communicative, and it needs an aware adult or older child to elicit relevance and intelligibility from the sounds and babblings that are made. The speed and efficiency with which babies and young children develop their vocabulary and extend their use of grammar — in environments where conversations take place naturally — is staggering. They seem to pick up all the oral clues and cues around them that they require to express their needs.

The spoken word sometimes seems to take on a magical property. We give it a power that it does not really possess. It is almost as if once words have been uttered, the ideas and opinions they express become fact, dangerous and painful 'truths' with a life of their own. If those ideas run counter to our own, it is as if they cannot be allowed to float free and be quietly reflected upon.

A failure to demolish ideas that are inconsistent with our own (particularly when our beliefs and ideas are strongly held) can make us uneasy and feel in some way wounded, devalued, threatened and insecure. Our responses in such situations are likely to be aimed at disconcerting and undermining the other speaker in an attempt to topple the viewpoint expressed and to assert one's own.

For many adults, such responses are the only strategies they have available. For, like children, without reflection we tend to react from habit rather than, in our maturity, to reflect and find a better way. *NG*

(Compiled from I'm Right, You're Wrong by Nigel Green.)

Valued lives —
Albert Einstein — *1879 -1955*

Albert Einstein is said to 'Rank with Galilei and Newton as one of the greatest conceptual revisers of man's understanding of the universe'. He was born in Ulm, Bavaria, on the 14th March 1879 of Jewish parent's, but took Swiss nationality in 1901 and began work at the Swiss patent office the following year.

At the same time, he worked on three 'world-shattering' papers on theoretical physics. His general theory of relativity was published in 1916. The theory was proved three years later when a solar eclipse gave English astronomer, Arthur Eddington, the opportunity to show that starlight measurably swerves as it passes through the heavier gravitation of the sun.

Such was the excitement that more than 100 books on relativity were published within a year, but Einstein claimed to be the only person in his circle *not* trying to win a $5,000 *Scientific American* prize. Einstein is reputed to have said, 'I don't believe I could do it.' His work on relativity won him the Nobel Prize for physics in 1922. But his popularity as the world's most famous scientist was not favourably received in his native Germany.

> ... he became a target for hatred. As a Jew, a liberal, a humanist, an internationalist, he attracted the enmity of nationalists and anti-Semites, abetted by a few jealous German physicists — an all too vigorous faction that Einstein called, while it was still possible to find this amusing, the Antirelativity Theory Company Ltd. *Time Magazine*

After professorships in Zurich and Prague, Einstein became director of the Kaiser Wilhelm Physical Institute in Berlin. But, with the rise of Hitler's power, he emigrated to Princetown New Jersey, where he lectured and later became an American citizen.

One aspect of his work, concerning the equation between mass, velocity and energy, was closely connected with work going on in the field of nuclear physics. In September 1939 Einstein wrote a 'momentous letter' to President Roosevelt pointing out that his theories could lead to the making of an atomic bomb, and that Germany, too, could be making one. After the war he urged international control of atomic weapons, for as Professor Bronowski said of him, 'He was full of humanity, pity and sense of enormous sympathy. He hated war, cruelty and hypocrisy, and above all he hated dogma — except that hate is not the right word for the sense of revulsion felt.'

Besides his lifelong passion for physics, Einstein was an enthusiastic, but 'never brilliant', amateur musician and played the violin in a trio with piano and 'cello. On commenting on his own 'rebelliousness' Einstein said, 'To punish me for my contempt for authority, Fate made me an authority myself.' He became an honorary associate of the Rationalist Press Association (RPA) and was also a member of the American Humanist Association (AHA). He lived in wonder of the creative energy that is everywhere in the cosmos and wrote in his autobiography:

The fairest thing we can experience is the mysterious. It is the fundamental emotion which stands at the cradle of true art and true science.

After his full but often solitarily happy life, Einstein died in his sleep on the 18th April 1955, leaving the world a greater understanding of its physical propensity.

* * * * *

Why I'm a Humanist— 4

I am a Humanist because I value reason above superstition, truth above obfuscation, fact above fiction, logic above magic. I am a Humanist because I believe morality is a social agreement for humanity's best conduct.

I am a Humanist because I value emotion, art, creativity, myth, legend, music and ritual, and regard these as human attributes and endeavours. I am a Humanist because I want to show others, especially the young, that principled, ethical, enquiring, compassionate and happy lives can be lived without reference to the supernatural.

I am a Humanist because when faced with the deep question of how life began and the astonishing complexities of the universe, I applaud the scientists and philosophers whose enquiries increase our knowledge; where gaps remain I happily put questions where the religious put their gods and their answers.

I am a Humanist because I am an atheist — I have no god-belief. I am a Humanist because I see human thought in progress, from pantheism, through polytheism and monotheism, to atheism and rationality. I am a Humanist because I celebrate my humanity. *MB*

All round the world

The Millennium celebrations are a distant memory of brief unity, when the 20th century — described as 'the bloodiest in human history' — moved inexorably into the 21st. The Accurist digital clock at Greenwich Observatory dictated passing time, while the international dateline and time zones spanned the world encompassing the globe like an invisible mesh. And as each zone heralded the change from one century to the next, celebrations great and small began.

One of the first was the tiny Pacific atoll renamed Millennium Island, where grass-skirted dancers marked the occasion, combining ancient dances with the modern technology of television. An hour later New Zealand was the first industrialised country to show that no millennium bug spoilt the festivities. Thousands gathered for a Maori ceremony, and a boy born at 12.01 was the first millennium baby.

Throughout the world, bells rang, fireworks exploded, people sang and danced. In China, where their new year would begin on the 5th of February, the president lit a ceremonial flame at China's Centenary Altar, as fireworks burst in the sky and Chinese pilots were airborne at midnight to show confidence in their technology. India largely ignored the Hindu calendar and celebrated in traditional western style.

Even Antarctica was included, when 30 Russian skydivers parachuted on to the ice. In Bethlehem 2000 doves were released, and in St Peter's Square the first rock concert to be staged was addressed by the Pope. Searchlights lit the sky and wheels began turning throughout successive midnights. Finally, islanders in Western Samoa celebrated 24 hours after their immediate neighbours, because of the vagaries of the international dateline.

A common bond of euphoria briefly held much of the world together. But as the new year progressed, all too quickly religious wars and civil conflict continued, perpetuating poverty, disease and unhappiness. Yet, somehow, the hope of a common bond still remains as countries and organisations struggle to reduce the causes that over-population, power and greed have caused. The future, it has been said, is in the hands of the younger generation — but the *present* belongs to everyone.

71

Active Humanism

Humanism is more than rationalism. It is more than atheism. If Humanism is to take its rightful place as a source of inspiration to humankind, as an alternative to theistic religion, and as a force for good in the world, then it must be about action; action to improve the human condition; to improve the lot of the poorest and most disadvantaged; to free them from the chains of poverty, ill-health, ignorance and superstition, and from the self-serving authoritarianism and neglect of the rich and powerful.

As an observer of international development co-operation, over many years, I have been dismayed by the extent to which national, political, religious and commercial considerations have been allowed to compromise practically all development assistance, both public and private. It could be argued that it doesn't matter what other purpose is being served provided the needy still benefit. There is growing evidence, however, to show that that response is misplaced. Much that passes for development assistance is misdirected and positively harmful to those it is supposed to help.

As Humanists our rationalist world-view can help us strip away the taboos, irrationality and assumptions of 'higher purpose' and focus on the real issues and their underlying causes. Working to eliminate the causes of poverty, war and disease can be far more cost-effective than responding — with however much good will — to the latest disaster to hit our TV screens. *Humanist Manifesto 2000* offers a framework for action. It combines a restatement of the philosophy underpinning Humanism with a list of practical issues that need to be addressed in working for a better world. Humanism has an important, if not key, role to play. It is easy to feel daunted when faced with the sheer scale of these problems. Every one of them is a major problem requiring co-ordinated effort on a global scale. Where does one start?

The answer, of course, is to think globally, but act locally. We can all lend our support to local and national organisations working to overcome these problems. Yes, Humanism needs its philosophy, but without action what value is its compassion? *RB*

(Compiled from Active Humanism, by Roy Brown in the December 2000/January 2001 International Humanist News.)

Background to the —

National Secular Society

The National Secular Society (NSS) was founded by Charles Bradlaugh in 1866 before he started his parliamentary career as a radical Liberal. He wanted to unite the various secular societies which had developed from the Owenite and Chartist movements.

One campaign he was involved with was the abolition of church rates. Until 1868, these were compulsory, and non-payment meant they could be legally enforced by having furniture or farm implements seized. This was bitterly resented by non-conformists and other 'dissenters', including the growing number of secularists and freethinkers. They joined together to campaign against this compulsory acquisition, until the rates were finally abolished. During the latter half of the nineteenth century NSS was the main freethought organisation in this country, with active branches holding hundreds of meetings a year. Many of these were held out of doors, either because hiring a hall was expensive or because hall owners refused to rent halls to 'such gatherings'.

Charles Bradlaugh believed that the spread of education would gradually and inexorably reduce the influence of religion. And some NSS branches held Sunday schools so that children, and in many cases adults too, could learn to read and write. As social life at that time was centred on the church or chapel it became necessary to provide an alternative for NSS members. Secular choirs, concert parties, dramatic societies, dances, picnics and excursions were organised, usually on Sundays when people had a holiday from work.

Alongside the social life, it was necessary to provide alternative ceremonies connected with life and death. Civil marriages became legal with the Marriage Act of 1836, but secular burial services were not legalised until 1880... A guide for the assistance of funeral officiants was issued in 1883. The following year, an agnostic surgeon, Sir Henry Thompson, founded the Cremation Society. *Foundations of Modern Humanism, William McIlroy*

Just before Charles Bradlaugh died, at the end of the nineteenth century, there were 100 NSS branches, with 100 outdoor weekly meetings held in London during reasonable weather. This was the height of 'organised secularism', with around 1,000 new members

73

joining NSS each year. But the growth of the leisure industry at that time ate away at both religious and secularist attendances. And as religion became less influential, so organised opposition to it waned.

However, NSS continued to campaign for the promotion of freethought, civil liberties and rational ethics. It took a leading part in the formation of the birth control movement and worked for a wide range of social reforms, including non-religious affirmation instead of the oath and the repeal of Sunday observance laws. Today, the society continues to promote voluntary euthanasia, race and sex equality, freedom of expression, the rights of minorities and animal welfare. It is especially concerned with the abolition of the blasphemy laws and minimising indoctrination in denominational schools. Key examples of remaining religious privilege include the state subsidy to the Church of England and its schools, and the twenty-six bishops' and archbishops' seats in the House of Lords.

NSS is the 'campaigning arm' of the secularist movement through issuing statements, holding public meetings and via the press and other media. An attempt to introduce a religious clause into the Family Law Divorce Bill was successfully opposed by the Society. The Catholic Church's continued opposition to abortion is carefully monitored, and the Society wishes to ensure that there is thorough, informed debate on Church and State separation.

The Freethinker is the monthly journal of NSS. It was founded in 1881 by G.W. Foote as a weekly paper, but in more recent years changed to its current monthly format. It is an effective antidote to superstition throughout the world and includes articles and commentary from a rationalist viewpoint.

Although the various branches of the Humanist/Secularist/ Freethought movement have the same fundamental belief in enhancing the natural world, and their aims and objectives overlap, each organisation has a different approach, which appeals to the wide membership, and fulfils a variety of functions within the general framework of freethought:

> They see themselves as colleagues rather than competitors in the broad struggle for freedom of thought and expression and from dogma and prejudice, and they welcome all forms of humanist thought and activity.

(See Bibliography on page 92 and Contacts on page 93.)

Real or pretend?

It would be perfectly possible to teach a very young child that a mobile phone is called a banana, and that is the name the child would accept until the difference is learnt. But if the child already knew both objects, it would be possible to *pretend* the banana was a phone and pretend to speak into it. In the first instance the child, without prior knowledge, would believe the inaccurate information. In the second instance the child would be capable of joining in and seeing it as a joke. And children love jokes.

John Earle (1628) described childhood as 'Innocence which time destroys'. Babies are innocent because they are not born 'bad' or 'naughty'. But they have potential. They pick up cues from their handlers and surroundings and, like sponges, absorb everything around them. Learning through seeing, hearing, doing, feeling and talking, slowly the narrow world of their immediate surroundings broadens. In this early-learning stage it would be possible to give the child almost any inaccurate information.

In early childhood children believe what they are told partly because, in their eyes, adults and older children *know everything* so what they say is unquestionably right, and partly because of the young child's limited knowledge for comparison. Between three and four they become more discerning and start to question. If the opportunity is available they will bombard anyone with questions and demand answers.

Father Christmas is accepted from an early age because he is seen as the giver of presents. Gradually, even if young children question his validity, they still *pretend* he is real just in case the presents stop coming! So they close their minds to the prospect of a grown man flying through the sky and coming down narrow chimneys. Many adults go along with the story as a bit of fun which has become a tradition. Ultimately, children, too, see it in this light — totally impossible but part of early childhood.

At primary school, children hear nursery rhymes, folk tales and bible stories which have become traditional. The stories are believed (unless told otherwise) because they are told by adults. Later, with wider knowledge of the world, many children come to see these stories as a mixture of fact and fiction — and just another part of early childhood.

Citizenship education

Education for Citizenship and the Teaching of Democracy is the official name of the citizenship project for schools. Having been involved with the Advisory Group from the beginning, I am hopeful that students and teachers will be enthusiastic when they become familiar with the material and examples of what primary and secondary schools have already done.

Pilot schemes in many areas were set up some two years ago, with School Councils discussing school democracy and community involvement. All schools were asked to think carefully about their democratic 'ways' before starting the programme, and there was full discussion of the aims and objects of the scheme with pupils and staff.

Citizenship education is not new. A Council for Education in World Citizenship was formed in 1939, and during the 1940s, teachers returning from the war were fired-up to teach about the United Nations and global issues. But the subject disappeared in the 1950s and occasionally briefly re-emerged.

The BHA has been contributing ideas to the present Advisory Group, chaired by Bernard Crick, since it formed in 1998. The programme's emphasis will lie in democracy, both at local and national level. Projects will include visits by MPs and councillors, with discussion about drugs, smoking, alcohol and local issues.

> 'Discussion inevitably involves controversial issues but we should not baulk at raising them,' the report says. And, 'Schools can only do so much but they should help to set values and attitudes towards active citizenship.'

Many primaries (which will receive light touch inspections) and secondaries (full OFSTED involvement) have examples of links to town halls, involvement in the local environment and visits. Teachers, youth workers and parents have become enthusiastic when shown the ideas and planning behind the programmes. After long years of campaigning, I remain hopeful of the outcome. BHA and many other organisations and individuals can be proud to have been involved. Apparently there is evidence of an increase in voting where youngsters have been exposed to some of the above initiatives. Let's hope this continues. *BT*

Local groups

Humanist groups have been springing up across the UK for over fifty years. Universities were a natural setting, where groups were prominent in the late 1940s. Then groups began to be formed in the larger towns. Tyneside Group (now a section of North East Humanists) started in the early fifties; Sutton Humanist Group formed in January 1956; and, equally successful, Brighton and Hove Humanists started two years later. Birmingham began in 1962 as more and more groups came into existence.

Each group expanded outwards, drawing in members from a wider area. Constitutions were prepared and programmes planned. Some groups formed, flowered and disappeared. Others amalgamated or divided into local area groups. Still more re-formed and expanded from earlier roots. Today's groups extend from Essex to Cornwall, through Wales, Northern Ireland and Scotland and across England from north to south. Some, however, cover so wide an area that smaller networks, under a county or regional umbrella, are being formed on a more local scale.

At first, groups were set up for social contact in members' homes, then many moved their focus out into the community. Most groups hold meetings in halls, pubs or community centres. Some put on displays in libraries, fairs or the market place. Others visit schools who request a speaker, and many groups now have a representative on the local Standing Advisory Council on Religious Education (SACRE). Others give talks on local radio, give press reports of their activities and voice controversial issues in local and national newspapers. Still more officiate at non-religious ceremonies, and all help charities either through the involvement of individual members or as group projects.

Besides donating to the Atheist Centre in Bombay, Sutton Humanists raise money for local charities by selling home-poduce and through their annual concert. Local recipients range from the Samaritans, a women's refuge and the Carers' centre. Lewisham group's book stalls help a variety of local, national and international charities. Cornwall help Macmillan nurses, and Devon members fill Aquaboxes with essential items for disaster areas. . .

Most groups are affiliated to BHA and receive regular mailings of *Humanist News* and literature published by BHA. A Group

Representatives Annual Meeting (GRAM) takes place in London, when representatives from across the country meet to discuss activities and glean ideas from other areas. Many groups produce their own newsletter which keeps members in touch and enables them to have a 'voice'. Some groups exchange newsletters and this, again, gives a useful interchange of ideas.

BHA's annual conference and regional conferences enable members (and non-members) to hear eminent speakers exploring aspects of many themes and give opportunity for discussing pertinent issues. They also allow valuable social contact.

Membership varies from a sprinkling to over 100 in each group. Not all members want to take part. Some are happy to join and receive regular newsletters in order to register their Humanist interest — which in turn helps the local group by strengthening its numbers. Others become actively involved, helping to organise events. Apart from the benefit of support and interest from like-minded people, one essential value of Humanist groups is to allow a Humanist *presence* to exist throughout the country, as a link in the chain of Humanist thought across the world.

* * * * *

Good news not bad please

The dramatic makes the headlines — murder; rape; wars; drugs; road, rail or air crashes; so-called 'sleaze' of eminent figures ... so day by day, week by week, negativism bombards us. It all happens and we cannot shut ourselves away from it, but this constant 'attack' has a destroying, defeatist effect, which for the sake of self survival ultimately makes us take important issues less seriously. An aggressive approach and dramatic headlines also highlight *un*dramatic events. There are seldom *discussions*, only *rows*, and 'bad' is assumed by implication. To agree with a different viewpoint is seen as a climb-down or U-turn and a sign of weakness, not a positive decision. People are said to be *furious* or *angry* if they even mildly disagree, and the bad that might have happened is pointed out, not the good that did. Most countries are not at war, millions of people do not get raped, murdered, or killed on the roads. Young people do an enormous amount of good, and people are working together for many community projects. More good news would stop us from being swamped with negativism and from switching off from the bad altogether.

I'll scratch your back...

In *The Time Machine*, H.G.Wells takes egocentricity to the extreme when the inventor sees a young woman fall into a swirling stream. Her friends, sitting on the bank, continue laughing and talking without stopping to help. But the inventor, coming from an earlier timescale, is baffled by their indifference and jumps in to save her.

Sometimes, we talk about the altruistic behaviour of one person helping another without reward, but can there be true altruism? To be completely altruistic we would give to the exclusion of ourselves, which is self-defeating and is not a characteristic of animals whose own survival is a basic instinct. It may sound selfish, but we help each other because deep down there is some benefit for us, even though it may be well disguised. It could be called self-motivation grounded in *reciprocal* altruism, since most species have evolved reciprocal behaviour patterns — grooming, warning, caring. The moment a baby is born it starts the battle for existence with 'self' the dominant reason for all its actions. People don't lose this egocentricity, they adapt it by co-operating with others, but in co-operating they are often, indirectly, helping themselves.

H.G. Wells showed a future society where people only helped themselves, but this meant they could not *expect* help in similar circumstances. If the culture grew that no one gave help, then no one would receive it, and ultimately all would be destroyed.

When the need to help is suddenly thrust upon us, we sometimes act instinctively. We don't usually think, 'If I help this person will someone help me?' But we would consider, even momentarily, whether our action would jeopardise our own life, if, for example, someone was drowning and we couldn't swim. We might even identify with the person's predicament and subconsciously empathise. If we walked away and did nothing how would we feel afterwards? Would we try to convince ourselves we couldn't have helped? Or would we think, supposing someone did that to me — or my family?

Another side to helping, is satisfaction. Being needed and being able to help is immensely satisfying. This in no way detracts from helpful behaviour; it is just as valid and just as essential. After all, everyone needs to give *and* to receive at some time.

Favourite music

I have a confession to make. I was born and brought up an atheist and I still am today. When I was a kid I can remember praying once or twice just to see if it worked, but of course it didn't. But I do love religious music. From Negro spirituals to Jewish cantors, from Russian Orthodox choirs to the West Gallery choirs of Hardy's time, the Shaker hymns to Sankey & Moody. As a teenager I can remember hearing for the first time Mahalia Jackson singing the carol *Silent Night* on the wireless. The power ... the passion. It was a spiritual experience.

Can you deny the beauty of *Amazing Grace?* Or even *The Old Rugged Cross?* One of my most favourite songs to this day is the hymn *Just a Closer Walk With Thee*, à la New Orleans jazz clarinettist, George Lewis. I have even recorded it, along with *Old Time Religion*, *I'll Fly Away* (To God's Celestial Shore) and *Oh Freedom* (I'll Go Home to My Lord and Be Free). Just because I sing about heaven, our lord and Jesus doesn't mean that I believe in them, any more than when I sing *I Saw Mummy Kissing Santa Clause* means that I believe in Father Christmas. *JL*

* * * * *

Capacity for opposites

We cannot have good without bad, right without wrong, happiness without unhappiness. But we are not born *good* or *bad*, nor do we know *right* from *wrong*. The concept of opposites gradually develops and may vary with different cultures. Yet we learn quickly to balance them. By appreciating the good moments, we are more able to cope with the bad, however hard they may be. Sometimes, when the 'bad' seems overwhelming, suddenly, often quite unexpectedly, a glimmer of 'good' appears — a kind act, an understanding comment, even just a friendly face.

We cope with unwanted situations in our own individual way. By drawing on memories or anticipating happier times, we get through the bad, feeling stronger for having done so. In this way we can more easily understand other people's problems, and apply our own personal experience when similar situations occur.

Exodus to Humanism

The distant origins are unknown of the small Hebrew tribe that had been nomadic, settled and then dispersed before returning to claim a more permanent home. But the culture surrounding its members grew. As time passed, invasions, the Diaspora and inter-marriage introduced 'new blood', increasing the numbers as the Jewish religion spread throughout the world.

Today, continuing to be Jewish, yet rejecting Jewish religious beliefs could pose problems. Once the religious aspect of being God's chosen people is rejected what helps each individual continue as part of their distinctly Jewish community?

One answer is in the deep seated culture that has developed over the years. In a similar way, a school or club 'culture' develops, and although the original focus may have gone, the culture of common experience lingers on and this is reinforced by continued expression.

From a non-Jewish perspective, I cannot know the depth of feeling experienced by the knowledge of another's 'Jewishness'. To me, being Jewish meant embodying the whole history of Jewish religious belief. But 'Jewishness' is partly an attitude of mind, which is shared by each family member growing up and absorbing certain traditions, in the same way that 'Welshness' or 'Cornishness' develops.

In attempting to find some answers, David Ibrey put together a collection of views, ideas, reasons and, in some cases, potted biographies from present day Humanists who were born into Jewish families but rejected the religious element of their culture. Together with his own reasons for his Humanist outlook, his book, *Exodus to Humanism*, explores how people came to make this decision. The writer is only partly Jewish, having had a non-believing Jewish father and a non-believing 'Christian' mother, although he states that it is descendancy from a Jewish mother's line that is important.

Whether sharing a traditional culture, in a rapidly changing world, is sufficient to hold that culture together will depend on its strength and whether it can be sustained without belief in the reason that created it.

(Exodus to Humanism by David Ibrey see Bibliography on page 92.)

Why I'm a Humanist — 5

I was brought up to attend church every Sunday. Aged six I joined the local High Anglican Choir, where I remained until I was sixteen. I was then confirmed by the Archbishop of Canterbury. In 1937 I left home to work as an indentured apprentice in London and lived at the YMCA hostel in Tottenham Court Road. My daily contacts were both the Christians and my fellow apprentices who were honest, hardworking and almost all irreligious. I bonded strongly with them and less with the YMCA as the years passed.

During the war I joined the navy and afterwards stayed on with a permanent commission, always taking part in official religious ceremonies. But I began to lose my conviction because of the contrast between the expressed belief of so many of my fellows and their life styles, which were noticeably less 'moral' (by my standards) than my own in all everyday matters. I felt unable to discuss this with anyone until I married a woman of Scottish Presbyterian background.

When our first child was born in 1951, we resisted all pressures for a christening and declared ourselves to be non-believers, with considerable resultant friction. The attitude of many of our devout relatives was so oppressive that we became convinced of the rightness of our decision. It was not until nearly twenty years later that we found the Humanist community. By then our children were all reared with no prescriptive religion, but freely studying and rejecting all the versions of Zen and similar youthful fashions. To my great satisfaction, they are all nice people and our grandchildren are developing into nice people too. I find this a great comfort because the decisions were not easy or simple at the time.

As Technical Director of an engineering company, where my fellow directors were of a like mind as myself, we had excellent employee relations. On two sites, with 135 employees, we had no disputes and never needed to dismiss anyone, so I recommend humanism for successful business management. I am glad to find more people with compatible ideas on how life should be lived and I find that the ten or so who have remained long term friends are all of this outlook, although none of them has joined any Humanist group. But it is the way they live that is important. *MG*

Humanism in India

India is a country steeped in the philosophies and superstitions of religion, which go hand in hand with the life of the people. Religion dominates every aspect of daily life. On street corners there are temples or mosques or shrines celebrating some god. By contrast, rationalism is also strong in India. *Carole Mountain*

The Indian Humanist movement has political, not religious, roots because of its founder M.N. Roy, who had been one of the leaders of the Congress Party. But he renounced his earlier political ties when he became convinced that freedom was the essence of human nature. In 1949 he founded the Indian Radical Humanist Association, one of the founder members of IHEU. He also founded the related Indian Renaissance Institute. The M.N. Roy Human Development Campus, of the Centre for the Study of Social Change at Mumbai (Bombay), keeps his memory alive.

Today, twelve organisations are members of IHEU and over thirty magazines are produced in ten languages including Hindi, Teluga, Malayalam, Gujarati, Bengali, Marathi, Oriya, Tamil and Punjabi, with eight magazines printed in English. *Humanscape* has a particular focus on voluntary work, and has subscribers from more than 200 cities and towns across India.

Humanist centres in many neighbourhoods throughout the country have been set up to give practical help by improving social conditions and education. They give health care and are helping to create a more sustainable life style. From the centres, neighbourhood newsletters are published which aim to promote 'communication on the common issues that neighbourhoods share'. Nearly 1,000,00 copies of different newsletters in various languages are distributed across the nation.

The Atheist Centre, which is supported by many international charities, is based at Vijayawada and has outreach programmes for integrated rural development in Andhra Pradesh (population eighty million). Health care, nutrition, basic education and economic and social help enable poor villages to become 'model communities', as examples for other villages. Through them, in over twenty years, thousands of families have been helped towards a happier, healthier life style.

(www.members.xoom.com/humanistindi)

Valued lives
Yehudi Menuhin — *1916-1999*

At the age of eighty-two Yehudi Menuhin was still conducting. His interest in music started when he was four and asked for a violin as soon as he heard one. He was born in New York to Russian-Jewish parents who encouraged his talent. By the age of seven he was appearing in public musical recitals and at thirteen performing in London and Paris. In 1932, when only sixteen, he recorded Elgar's violin concerto, conducted by the seventy-five year old composer. Although he is regarded by many as the greatest violinist, he will also be remembered for his humanitarian interests. It was his deep understanding and appreciation of music that led to his belief that music stood for a way of overcoming the divide that exists between many people and cultures.

Yehudi Menuhin was on BHA's Advisory Council when it was established in 1963. In 1970 his interest in humane causes came to the fore by spreading and teaching a love of music all over the world. He founded a school in Surrey for musically gifted children, 'to nurture the talents of future generations of musicians', and an institution that encouraged the teaching of music to under-privileged children in Europe. He also set up an organisation for arranging concerts in prisons. He became a British citizen in 1980. His musical interests did not remain static, for he was always learning, and in looking for spontaneous improvisation he joined the jazz musician Stephane Grappelli in a remarkable recording of *Tea for Two*. This was another way in which he used music to stretch across the divide.

After his death, the *Independent* said:

> Britain owes Yehudi Menuhin a great debt and more than a moments thought. What he brought this country was not only a considerable musicianship, but a real devotion to public causes and musical education. His services to building bridges with Germany just after the war, the Communist world during the cold war, and the Third World required courage and imagination. He was also a great humanist both in his belief in the healing power of art and his willingness to give his all to it.

Yehudi Menuhin will long be remembered for his musical talent and his humanitarian interests.

Background to the —
Humanist Housing Association

The Humanist Housing Association (HHA) started as the Ethical Union Housing Association. It was registered in late 1954 and floated on the 24th January 1955. It was founded by the Ethical Union (soon to become the British Humanist Association) with the object of providing sheltered housing for elderly people at a time when sheltered, individual flats were seldom provided. The idea followed the Dutch Humanist League's scheme for purpose built well-planned flats, with social amenities and common rooms.

A recommended architect set to work on plans to adapt the first sheltered housing scheme, Burnet House, into fourteen bedsits with kitchenettes. Bathroom facilities were shared, although central heating — a luxury at that time — was provided. The house was opened in 1957 and named after two of the founding members, Lindsay and Moira Burnet.

At the same time that the housing association was developing, BHA was emerging from Ethical Union and Rationalist Press roots. The widening provision of HHA was one of the ways in which Humanism was working in the community.

The second scheme, purpose-built Blackham House in Wimbledon, was completed in 1963. It was divided into twenty flatlets, each with its own small kitchen. Showers and bathrooms were still shared, but the flats now had their own lavatory and hand basin. Rose Bush Court in Hampstead, also purpose-built, followed in 1968 with twenty-seven fully self-contained flats. Both houses were named after members of the original committee, that continued to manage the HHA on a voluntary basis, although paid Wardens were appointed.

By 1970 the demand for sheltered housing was outstripping supply, but the property boom in 1972 meant building and land prices had escalated. Nevertheless, Rose Bush Court was extended to create a further thirty self-contained, one-bedroomed sheltered flats. After the 1974 Housing Act HHA rapidly developed and could no longer be managed by a voluntary committee. In 1976, Robert Morton House was built, providing a further forty-six flats.

HHA now looked into the provision of refuges for battered women and alternative housing for those with mental health problems. Extending out from London into Kent, the Association began building sheltered flats and supported flats at Pembury. Later twenty-four general needs flats were built. In the meantime, Balmoral House, at Tunbridge Wells, was converted into a residential care home for the frail elderly, and two houses nearby provided over fifty more sheltered flats. Spreading into Surrey, Hertfordshire, Essex, Middlesex and Cambridge more purpose-built sheltered flats were provided. A feature of all the houses was their well-designed gardens where residents could walk, sit and talk and hold the occasional garden party.

A second residential care home, Moira Burnet House, was opened in 1985, with a section for sheltered accommodation. The following year, HHA took over the management of sheltered flats owned by the National Council for Carers and their Elderly Dependents (later the Carers National Association). Increasingly they managed further sheltered housing in conjunction with specialist agencies, and by the 1990s managed over 1,000 units, including special needs, residential care, leasehold flats and housing schemes on behalf of other housing associations.

From the outset HHA aimed at providing high quality, value-for-money, affordable services to meet local needs and to maximise choice for residents, enabling them to have as much independence as possible. The policy was to treat people with dignity and always to respect confidentiality in all aspects of the work. Feedback was important as well as acting upon it.

Although HHA became independent from BHA, the founding principles lived on through the comprehensive equal opportunities policy towards applicants for housing, the tenants, residents and staff, and in the services provided.

A marked increase in the UK population above retirement age, the number of frail elderly people and the fact that many older people were living alone, meant that HHA extended the options available and developed flexible services which could adapt to growing needs. Putting their plans into practice was always a team effort, involving working with local communities, local authorities and health and social services to meet local needs in the most effective and efficient way.

HHA started as a small concern because a local need was realised, then it grew and grew, expanding to meet new demands. But in 2000, with continued changes, HHA was taken over by a larger housing association. It is hoped that the care and humanity that enabled HHA to thrive will live on into the future.

Other people are different

There are 100 billion stars in our galaxy, and 100 billion galaxies: which amounts to an awful lot of stars. Around a lot of them there will be planets orbiting and, so say some, it is inconceivable that some of those planets will not be so adjusted as to make them capable of producing life as we know it.

Even if the odds are greater than those against winning the National Lottery, there should still be one or two winners. But statistics are one thing, hard evidence another. That is why the news that rock sample ALH 84001, showing a primitive life form to have existed on Mars some four billion years ago, has been shaking the imagination of the whole world. And it is why an American astronomer caused such a stir when he announced the discovery of two stars a mere 32 million light years away, that appeared to have orbiting planets that might just conceivably have oceans and rain, two prerequisites of life. But neither of these discoveries indicates any glimmering of intelligence.

How would we react to intelligent forms from other worlds, particularly as, as seems probable, they would be more advanced than us? We could, relative to them, be in the stone age. Even if they were friendly they could swamp us as surely as the Western World has swamped aboriginal culture here.

All this makes me reflect on how tribal are our instincts. We turn inwards to the family, religion, union, any tribal grouping of which we acquire membership, and then promptly turn aggressively outwards. Other people are different and must be either rejected or converted to be like us. Religions seem to be liable to these tribal instincts, and whatever good they do within their tribes is often outweighed by mayhem generated outside.

Two-way communication is the essential for understanding, and that depends on both sides being rational. Probes sent into space, on the off chance they might be picked up by intelligent life, contain scientific data on the human form and mathematical formulas, not theological argument and offers of redemption. It is rational minds that we expect to pick up and such strangers, whatever their outer form, will not be different. Humanists offer, too, this same rational meeting of minds to all fellow members of the human tribe on *this* earth. *JE*   *(First broadcast on local radio.)*

The marketing gap

Humanism is a brilliant product, a life-enriching philosophy urgently needed to combat life-destroying terrorism, drugs, hijacking, hostage-taking, vandalism, racial strife, environmental pollution, fear of death, undeserved guilt and over-population. Humanism is a set of honourable values, good guidelines (not dogma) for human behaviour. But how can people find Humanists if Humanists do not reveal themselves? Religionists talk to the whole world. Humanists talk mostly to each other.

In the course of ordinary daily chit-chat, Christians will say, "I am a born-again Christian", "The Bible says...", "Praise be to God!". How often do Humanists create an opportunity to discuss the subject by saying, "I find the Humanist viewpoint on that subject interesting." Or "I disagree with that idea from the Humanist standpoint." Or "You'd make a good Humanist."

The old eternal questions have been answered.

Q. How did we get here? **A**. We evolved.

Q. Why do we live? **A**. Because we were born and have not yet died. Because a male and female mated.

Q. What is the purpose of life? **A**. Any purpose you choose to give it.

The new questions are: How can we get more satisfaction, more accomplishment and joy out of life without damaging others? How can we make a profit without causing others to suffer a loss? Humanism offers some good answers.

Fundamentalists are backing themselves into a corner, unable to evolve because they don't believe in it, unable to meet challenging needs because their rules are absolute and unquestionable. New Age enthusiasts are rejecting the dictatorial, violent, jealous gods of the Bible, Koran and Talmud, and are seeking help from extra-terrestials, channelers and spirits, not to mention gemstones with miraculous powers and subliminal self-hypnosis cassettes.

Perhaps ordinary laziness is the reason why Humanists don't advertise their product. But the time is ripe. Everybody is looking for a mind set that will make life worth living. We've got the ready-made product. What are we waiting for? *KC*

(From Kate Contos' article in Honest to Goodness? - see Bibliography.)

Feeling mellow

I sat and wondered what to offer you [*in my broadcast*] today, finding it difficult to concentrate. The sun was casting long shadows over the garden. The cats had spent several hours stretched out on the shed roof watching the world go by through half-open eyes. The sparrows were having a loud argument about roosting space in the hedge. The virginia creeper had turned red when I wasn't paying attention. Nothing much had happened all day except that those bits of me which become tired and tense were gradually unravelling themselves. Bliss.

Periods of rest and recuperation are essential to everyone. It seems to me that many people regard leisure, like the rest of their lives, as something to seek at full tilt, no expense spared; it doesn't count unless you've driven miles to do it, spent money and worn yourself out in the process.

Recently, a busy career woman complained to me that she couldn't cope with juggling her commitments any more. She was trying to keep several balls in the air at the same time. I suggested she drop one or two and find some time for relaxation.

"What a good idea," she said.

She announced she would find someone to give her some therapeutic massage, which meant finding a masseur, driving to wherever they were and forking out more of the money she'd worked so hard to earn. Her idea of relaxation sounded stressful to me — and maybe it's my age, but why do so many people seem to spend their leisure time making a lot of noise?

Relaxation is about letting go; letting go of the feeling that you are indispensable; letting go of the guilt about failing to meet other people's expectations; letting go of all your anxieties; letting go of the feeling that you ought to be doing something without knowing quite what; allowing yourself just to *be*.

William Henry Davies wrote, 'What is this life if, full of care, we have no time to stand and stare?' What indeed? *MN*

(This is one of a collection of Thoughts for the Day, broadcast by BBC Radio Suffolk, see Bibliography for details of a collection of the talks.)

Contributors

Peter Astwood - trained as a physicist; in later life became a teacher, then Head of the Mathematics Department in a large comprehensive school; now retired; variety of interests including: art, ecology, literature, rambling.

Maureen Berry - retired teacher of English; writes book reviews and magazine features; married with two adult sons; founder member of South Somerset Humanists; now lives in Devon where she organises the Torbay area network for Devon Humanists.

Roy Brown - IHEU Growth and Development Committee; founder and former chairman World Population Foundation of the Netherlands; board member International Foundation for Population & Development Switzerland.

Brenden Butler - retired local government officer; second career as a farmer; enjoyed 'the freedom of the skies' as an amateur pilot in his light aircraft; his book, *The Beckoning Sky*, tells of his great enthusiasm for flying.

Kate Contos - freelance writer and broadcaster in New Zealand; American citizen; advertised for people with inquiring, agnostic minds, together they set up the Hawkes Bay Freethinker Group.

John Eadle - member of South Somerset Humanists; served in the RNVR during World War 2; then had a career in the Civil Service; classed himself a humanist over twenty years ago.

Martin Gilbert - 30 years in Royal Navy; Technical Director of an engineering firm; recommends Humanism for successful business management;"rare not to receive a good response to tolerance and respect for others"; company chairman in 1978.

Nigel Green - teacher; lecturer; Open University tutor; Curriculum Development Co-ordinator with Overseas Development Administration; LEA Adviser; writer and educational consultant.

John Langford - brought up as an atheist; founder member of Cornwall Humanists; non-religious ceremonies officiant; folk singer who has, "Now joined the ranks of OAPs!"

Richard Lovis - has lived in Plymouth all his life, where he taught for 24 years before early retirement; four years teaching 'English as a Foreign Language'; recently retired as Unitarian Lay Pastor.

Roger McCallister - degree in geology; qualified as town planner;

30 years planning officer in local government; currently part-time planning adviser for National Trust; secretary Devon Humanists; married with son and daughter and one grandson.

Carole Mountain - born in Guildford; career in radiography, then teaching; magistrate since 1984, first in Telford then Exeter; founder member of Manchester Humanists, then Devon Humanists; ceremonies officiant and Regional Co-ordinator.

Margaret Nelson - successful single parent (adult son); artist and designer; former teacher and journalist; currently Humanist officiant, speaker and broadcaster; council tenants' representative for local housing management.

Stephen Park - grew up in Newcastle; trained as an artist; now has small business 'edge of Dartmoor' making jewelry with his wife.

Richard Paterson - OU graduate; University of Wales Counselling Studies Diploma; ceremonies officiant then full time manager of Cruse Bereavement Care in Wales; former BHA Chair; helped re-establish Cardiff Humanists; married with 3 daughters and 2 sons.

Henrietta Quinnell - BA FSA MIFA archaeologist; early retirement from Exeter University running adult education programme; now concentrating on research into the pre-history of Britain.

Claire Rayner - OBE; her nursing career led to midwifery then paediatrics; after marriage she became a journalist, broadcaster and counsellor and writer of educational, medical and children's books; President of BHA from 1999; honorary associate of RPA.

Barbara Smoker - brought up a Roman Catholic; overseas wartime service in Royal Navy; at 26 renounced Catholicism for Humanism; active in social campaigns; president of the NSS from 1971 to 1999; ceremonies officiant and trainer.

Bryan Steane - began working life as an engineer in the steel industry; changed course and became a history teacher, then Principal Axe Valley Community College; interests: architecture, travel, music, film, dance, drama, making violins/'cellos, politics.

Bob Tutton - retired primary school headteacher; became a Humanist in 1960s; involved with Education Association, BHA, NUT, Advisory Group for Citizenship Education, Friends of the Earth, CASE; married with two sons and two grandchildren.

Jane Wynne Willson - retired teacher; actively involved with the Humanist movement, locally, nationally and internationally; has written books on Humanist ceremonies and parenting.

Bibliography

Blackham, H. J., 1968 *Humanism*, Penguin

Carson, Rachel, 1999 *Silent Spring*, Penguin ISBN 0140273719

Collins, Nigel, 2000 *Seasons of Life:* poetry and prose for secular ceremonies, Rationalist Press Association

Contos, Kate, 1992 Humanism and the Marketing Gap in *Honest to Goodness?*, The Humanist Society of New Zealand ISBN 0473016672

Darwin, Charles, *Origin of Species,* Penguin Classics ISBN 010432051

Voyage of the Beagle, Penguin Classics ISBN 014043268X

Dawkins, Richard, 1988 *The Blind Watchmaker,* Penguin ISBN 0140144811

1996 *Climbing Mount Improbable,* Viking ISBN 0670850187

1995 *River Out of Eden:* a Darwinian view of life, Phoenix ISBN 1857994051

1995 *The Selfish Gene*, Oxford ISBN 019286025

1998 *Unweaving the Rainbow,* Penguin ISBN 071399214X

Forster, E. M., 1999 *What I Believe,* G.W. Foote & Co.

Fowler, Jeaneane, 1999 *Humanism:* Beliefs and Practices, Sussex Academic Press ISBN 1898723702

Graham, Frank, 1972 *Since Silent Spring,* Pan/Ballantine

Herrick, Jim, (editor) 2001 *Rationalism in the Twenty-First Century,* Rationalist Press Association ISBN 0301001022

Hobson, Alfred and Jenkins, Neil, 1994 *Modern Humanism*: living without religion, Adelphi Press ISBN 1856541118

Humphrys, John, 2000 *Devil's Advocate* Arrow, ISBN 099279657

Huxley, Julian, (ed) 1965 *The Humanist Frame,* Allen & Unwin

Ibry, David, 1999 *Exodus to Humanism*: Jewish identity without religion, Prometheus ISBN 1573922676

Kelly, Kevin, 1995 *Out of Control,* Fourth Estate ISBN 1857023080

Kennedy, Ludovic, 1999 *All in the Mind,* Hodder & Stoughton ISBN 0340680636

Kishlansky, Mark et al, 1991 *Civilization in the West,* Harper Collins ISBN 0673463869

Knight, Margaret, 1955 *Morals Without Religion,* Dobson

Knight, Margaret and Herrick, Jim, (editor) 1996 *Humanist*

Anthology, Rationalist Press Association ISBN 0301940010

Lamont, Corliss, 1982 *The Philosophy of Humanism,* Frederick Ungar

Leakey, Richard, 1981 *The Making of Mankind,* Michael Joseph ISBN 0718119312

1994 *The Origin of Humankind,* Weidenfeld & Nicholson ISBN 0297815032

Mason, Marilyn, 2000 *The Thinkers' Guide to Life* [quotations], Rationalist Press Association ISBN 0301000026

McIlroy, William, 1995 *Foundations of Modern Humanism,* Sheffield Humanist Society ISBN 0952564408

Nelson, Margaret, 2000 *Humanist Thought for the Day:* given on Radio Suffolk, Suffolk Humanists

Ratcliffe, S.K., 1955 *The Story of South Place,* Watts & Co.

Shattuck, Roger, 1980 *The Forbidden Experiment,* Secker & Warburg

Smoker, Barbara, 1998 *Humanism:* an update for the new millennium, BHA ISBN 0706231465

Wynne Willson, Jane, 1999 *Funerals Without God,* BHA

1999 *New Arrivals:* non-religious baby namings, BHA

1999 *Parenting Without God,* BHA

1999 *Sharing the Future:* non-religious weddings, BHA

Humanist Dipper, 1991 BHA

Key Figures in Humanism, 1994 BHA

Humanism — The Great Human Detective Story (video), BHA

A Short Course on Humanism, 2001 BHA

Contacts

BHA -39 Moreland Street London EC1V 8BB
info@humanism.org.uk www.humanism.org.uk
0207 324 3060

IHEU - 39 Moreland Street London EC1V 8BB
office-iheu@iheu.org www.iheu.org.uk
0207 490 8468

IHEU: humanism@iheu.org   <www.iheu.org>
NSS: kpw@secularism.org.uk   <www.secularism.org.uk>
RPA: info@rationalist.org.uk   <www.rationalist.org.uk>
SPES: library@ethicalsoc.org.uk   <www.ethicalsoc.org.uk>

Index